Jungian Psychoanalysis

T0386407

Jungian Psychoanalysis: A Contemporary Introduction provides a concise overview of analytical psychology as developed by Carl Jung.

Mark Winborn offers a succinct introduction to the key elements of Jung's conceptual model and method, as well as an outline of the major transitions, critiques, and debates that have emerged in the evolution of analytical psychology. Similarities and differences between analytical psychology and other psychoanalytic orientations are also identified. This approach allows those who already have familiarity with the Jungian model to expand their understanding, while also providing an accessible map of the field to those with limited exposure to these concepts.

Psychoanalysts, therapists, students, and instructors of all levels of experience will benefit from this unique introduction to the Jungian model of psychoanalysis.

Mark Winborn (PhD, NCPsyA) is a Jungian psychoanalyst/clinical psychologist. He is a training/supervising analyst of the Inter-Regional Society of Jungian Analysts and the C.G. Jung Institute of Zurich. He is the author of *Interpretation in Jungian Analysis: Art and Technique* and *Beyond Persona: On Individuation and Beginnings with Jungian Analysts* (with Lavinia Țânculescu-Popa), as well as two additional books.

"This book brilliantly outlines and integrates a breadth of understanding of Jung's depth psychology in concert with contemporary psychoanalytic theory and practice. A much needed and timely opus, this volume is a feast of psychoanalytic knowledge punctuated with moving personal clinical experience and wisdom. A gem for Jungians and all those devoted to psyche."

Ronnie Landau, Jungian psychoanalyst, President – CNASJA, past-President – Philadelphia Association of Jungian Analysts

"This volume, in the series Routledge Introductions to Contemporary Psychoanalysis, gives a brilliant introduction to the classical concepts in Jungian psychoanalysis while at the same time integrating important debates in the field of analytical psychology as well as linking to concepts from other psychoanalytic perspectives. I find the book most inspiring, and I highly recommend it for all those looking for an excellent contemporary introduction to Jungian psychoanalysis."

Misser Berg, Jungian analyst, Denmark, President of the International Association for Analytical Psychology

"A welcome introduction to the richness and significance of Jungian thought. Especially welcome at this time, as Jung's vision of psychic reality delineates important components of world political impasse as well as depths of group and individual psychology. The author opens flexible dynamic currents between therapy schools enhancing what therapeutic communities can offer. Jung has been a generative background presence in the therapy field and Mark Winborn's foreground presentation enhances access, knowledge, and growth of experience."

Michael Eigen, PhD, psychoanalyst and author of *Contact with the Depths, The Challenge of Being Human*, and *Faith, The Birth of Experience*

"The development of dialogue between analytical psychology and contemporary psychoanalysis is essential for a deeper understanding of the multidimensional picture of the unconscious. Mark Winborn's book is an excellent contribution to the development of a poly-theoretical perspective for exploring the complexity of the psyche's manifestations and to the understanding of the specificity of the Jungian approach."

Gražina Gudaitė, PhD, Professor at Vilnius University, Lithuania, Vice-President of the International Association for Analytical Psychology, and Editor of *Exploring Core Competencies in Jungian Psychoanalysis: Research, Practice and Training*

Routledge Introductions to Contemporary Psychoanalysis

Aner Govrin, PhD
Series Editor

Tair Caspi, PhD
Executive Editor

Yael Peri Herzovich
Assistant Editor

Routledge Introductions to Contemporary Psychoanalysis is one of the prominent psychoanalytic publishing ventures of our day. It will comprise dozens of books that will serve as concise introductions dedicated to influential concepts, theories, leading figures, and techniques in psychoanalysis covering every important aspect of psychoanalysis.

The length of each book is fixed at 40,000 words.

The series' books are designed to be easily accessible to provide informative answers in various areas of psychoanalytic thought. Each book will provide updated ideas on topics relevant to contemporary psychoanalysis – from the unconscious and dreams, projective identification and eating disorders, through neuropsychoanalysis, colonialism, and spiritual-sensitive psychoanalysis. Books will also be dedicated to prominent figures in the field, such as Melanie Klein, Jaque Lacan, Sandor Ferenczi, Otto Kernberg, and Michael Eigen.

Not serving solely as an introduction for beginners, the purpose of the series is to offer compendiums of information on particular topics within different psychoanalytic schools. We ask authors to review a topic but also address the readers with their own personal views and contribution to the specific chosen field. Books will make intricate ideas comprehensible without compromising their complexity.

We aim to make contemporary psychoanalysis more accessible to both clinicians and the general educated public.

Aner Govrin
Editor

For more information about this series, please visit: https://www.routledge.com/Routledge-Introductions-to-Contemporary-Psychoanalysis/book-series/ICP

Jungian Psychoanalysis

A Contemporary Introduction

Mark Winborn

LONDON AND NEW YORK

Designed cover image: © Michal Heiman, *Asylum 1855–2020*, "The Sleeper" (video, psychoanalytic sofa and Plate 34), exhibition view, Herzliya Museum of Contemporary Art, 2017.

First published 2024
by Routledge
4 Park Square, Milton Park, Abingdon, Oxon OX14 4RN

and by Routledge
605 Third Avenue, New York, NY 10158

Routledge is an imprint of the Taylor & Francis Group, an informa business

© 2024 Mark Winborn

British Library Cataloguing-in-Publication Data
A catalogue record for this book is available from the British Library

Library of Congress Cataloging-in-Publication Data
Names: Winborn, Mark, author.
Title: Jungian psychoanalysis : a contemporary introduction / Mark Winborn.
Description: Abingdon, Oxon ; New York, NY : Routledge, 2024. |
Series: Routledge introductions to contemporary psychoanalysis | Includes
bibliographical references and index. |
Identifiers: LCCN 2023010100 (print) | LCCN 2023010101 (ebook) |
ISBN 9781032121956 (hardback) | ISBN 9781032121932 (paperback) |
ISBN 9781003223511 (ebook)
Subjects: LCSH: Jungian psychology. | Psychoanalysis.
Classification: LCC BF173.J85 W5283 2024 (print) | LCC BF173.J85 (ebook) |
DDC 150.19/54--dc23/eng/20230501
LC record available at https://lccn.loc.gov/2023010100
LC ebook record available at https://lccn.loc.gov/2023010101

ISBN: 978-1-032-12195-6 (hbk)
ISBN: 978-1-032-12193-2 (pbk)
ISBN: 978-1-003-22351-1 (ebk)

DOI: 10.4324/9781003223511

Typeset in Times New Roman
by Taylor & Francis Books

Contents

Figures

Introduction

I am delighted to have received an invitation from Aner Govrin to contribute a volume on contemporary Jungian psychoanalysis to the series Introductions to Contemporary Psychoanalysis. Not only is it an honor to be invited, but the overall philosophy of the series is in keeping with my own views about psychoanalysis. My initial interest in psychoanalysis developed through the work of Carl Gustav Jung and analytical psychology. I was attracted by his approach to spiritual experience, emphasizing it as a significant and meaningful part of life, as well as his capacity to cast psychological theory within a broad cultural background.

However, early in my analytic training, I was exposed to other psychoanalytic schools of thought through three supervisors/teachers who held poly-theoretical orientations to clinical work which complemented and expanded their foundation in the Jungian model. Because they were able to draw from other perspectives and make contrasts between Jungian concepts and other theoretical frameworks, I experienced them as having a more differentiated and nuanced understanding of Jung, while also having a more diverse perspective on clinical phenomena than my supervisors and instructors who were primarily focused exclusively on ideas from analytical psychology. Casting a broad net within the world of psychoanalytic ideas has remained a significant part of my journey for thirty years. Therefore, contributing to this series is an important, organic part of my journey.

Through the initial influence of my supervisors, and by following my own curiosity, I developed a working knowledge of self psychology, the Kleinian perspective, object relations, Bion, intersubjectivity,

DOI: 10.4324/9781003223511-1

and the relational perspective. While I routinely draw on concepts and techniques from all these perspectives, I find the work of Wilfred Bion and other post-Bionian writers to be the most influential complement to my Jungian background, so much so that I now consider my approach to be a Jungian–Bionian hybrid.

C.G. Jung and analytical psychology have a complex and interesting position within the broader psychoanalytic context. On the one hand, even though the Freud–Jung split occurred in 1913, over one hundred years ago, there remains a strong element of resistance from many in the Jungian world around incorporating ideas from other schools of psychoanalysis. While there are many who are comfortable integrating other psychoanalytic ideas and techniques, many still adhere to the perspective that analytical psychology is cut from a different cloth than other models of psychoanalysis and wish to avoid having Jung's model 'contaminated' by other models which are historically rooted in Freud's conceptions of the psyche.

Similarly, many in the psychoanalytic world still harbor reservations about Jung and Jungian analysts dating back to the split between Jung and Freud and the subsequent efforts by Freud and his inner circle to discredit Jung and his theories (Grosskurth 1991). Many in the psychoanalytic world perceive Jung as too mystical or are confused by Jung's dense references to seemingly arcane sources from mythology, alchemy, and Gnosticism to support his theories and illustrate his case material. While Jung's language and references may seem opaque to those new to his approach, the language and style of Melanie Klein, Jacques Lacan, or Wilfred Bion are also often difficult to absorb for those new to their work until a degree of immersion has occurred.

Yet, some of the psychoanalytic world's resistance to Jung has diminished over the past few decades. Anne Alvarez, a Kleinian analyst, acknowledges this shift:

> We need the psychoanalytic perspective to help us see the acorn in the oak tree, the baby in the child or the lost breast in the child's cuddly soft teddy. But we may need the developmentalists and Jung's perspective to help us to see the oak tree in the acorn, the man the child will become and is in the process of becoming.
>
> (1992, p. 177)

Samuels (1996, p. 472) summarizes the evolution in contemporary psychoanalysis which has permitted greater receptivity to Jung, "Post-Freudian psychoanalysis has gone on to revise, repudiate, and extend many of Freud's seminal ideas. … Many of the central issues and features of contemporary psychoanalysis are reminiscent of positions taken by Jung in earlier years." This shift is also reflected in an observation by Freudian scholar Paul Roazen, "Few responsible figures in psychoanalysis would be disturbed today if an analyst were to present views identical to Jung's in 1913" (1976, p. 272). Robert Wallerstein[1] provides an even broader assessment of the situation in terms of the relationship between Freud and Jung and ultimately between the psychoanalytic community and analytical psychology:

> There are people who are saying today, and I think they're right, if the Jungian viewpoint had arisen today, it would be accommodated within the body of psychoanalysis the way Kohut has been, rather than Jungians feeling they had to leave. The kind of unity that Freud tried to impose was an impossible one because it demanded a real orthodoxy.
>
> (quoted in Hunter 1994, p. 333)

Brown (2018) highlights the need for greater dialogue between analytical psychology and contemporary psychoanalysis. The work of reconciling analytical psychology and psychoanalysis began with a group of psychoanalytically informed Jungians in post-World War II London,[2] under the influence of Michael Fordham. Jungian analysts who integrate psychoanalytic ideas and place greater emphasis on early life development have come to be referred to as the 'developmental school' of analytical psychology (Samuels 1985) and this orientation has become an influential perspective in analytical psychology.

In keeping with the philosophy of this series, Introductions to Contemporary Psychoanalysis, the purpose of this volume is to provide an overview of the development and core conceptual themes in Jungian psychoanalysis for those who are less familiar with Jung's model. In addition, this volume addresses the relationship between Jung's ideas and similar ideas from other schools of psychoanalytic thought, as well as highlighting the elements of Jung's model which may complement other psychoanalytic perspectives. This volume also provides a forum for me to share some of my reflections on being a contemporary Jungian psychoanalyst working from a poly-theoretical perspective.

Chapter 1 provides a succinct history of analytical psychology, the early relationship between Freud and Jung, and how the conflicts that emerged in that relationship shaped the development of analytical psychology. I also highlight the uneasy relationship over the decades between psychoanalysis and analytical psychology. Finally, I outline the major theoretical shifts and orientations that have emerged as analytical psychology has evolved since its inception.

The second chapter, "Aims and Attitudes in Jungian Psychoanalysis," highlights the primary focus or goal of Jungian psychoanalysis, particularly Jung's concept of individuation. In this chapter, the symbolic attitude, consciousness, teleological influences, and the place of the unknown are also addressed. The chapter concludes with an exploration of the analytic relationship in Jungian psychoanalysis and the theoretical rapprochement occurring between analytical psychology and psychoanalysis as concepts similar to Jung's are emerging in other psychoanalytic orientations.

Archetypes and the collective unconscious are the focus of Chapter 3. Archetypes and the collective unconscious are the most significant conceptual aspects of analytical psychology which differentiate Jungian psychoanalysis from other schools of psychoanalysis, therefore they are central to understanding Jung's theoretical model. There is also a vibrant debate going on within Jungian psychoanalysis about contemporary interpretations of these concepts. These critiques are outlined in Chapter 3.

Chapter 4 focuses exclusively on Jung's theory of complexes and the clinical application of the theory. In the chapter, research on complexes and recent reinterpretations and expansions of Jung's original theory are discussed. I also highlight the strong parallels between Jung's complex theory and object relations theory.

In Chapter 5, I survey Jungian dream theory and praxis. I outline Jung's orientation to dream theory and his associative-dramatic process of dream interpretation, as well as discussing the differences between Jung and Freud regarding dreams. Additionally, I outline some of the different approaches that have emerged within analytical psychology, such as those of Robert Bosnak and James Hillman. Finally, I discuss the similarities and differences between Jungian approaches to dreams and the approach of Wilfred Bion.

The majority of the other key concepts in analytical psychology are addressed in Chapter 6. Here I discuss Jung's conceptualization of libido, symbols, the transcendent function, typology, and synchronicity.

Chapter 7 is devoted to Jungian perspectives on defenses and psychopathology. This chapter discusses the relative lack of focus on defense processes in analytical psychology and the issues that emerge from that lack of emphasis. I also discuss uniquely Jungian contributions to the theory of defenses as well as Jung's conceptualization of psychopathology which emphasizes the whole personality of the patient and the role of one-sidedness in the patient's conscious position in terms of the development of psychopathology.

The role of technique in Jungian psychoanalysis is discussed in Chapter 8. As with defenses, much of the Jungian analytic community has held long standing reservations in terms of the role of technique in analysis. The limitations that emerge from these reservations are explored, as well as the rationale behind the reservations. The remainder of the chapter focuses on Jungian perspectives on the analytic frame, transference/countertransference analysis, interpretation, and active imagination.

Chapter 9 provides an overview of Jungian psychoanalytic training. Particular emphasis is placed on the differences between Jungian analytic training and training from other schools of psychoanalytic thought, especially the Jungian emphasis on the immersive study of mythology, fairy tales, religious systems, and alchemy. Other ancillary subject matter that is not found in other psychoanalytic training settings is also described.

My reflections on my own practice as a clinical psychologist and contemporary Jungian psychoanalyst are the focus of Chapter 10, i.e., an abbreviated analytic credo. In this chapter, I highlight the elements of the Jungian approach I value and the areas of

Jungian psychoanalysis which I disagree with or do not find valuable. I also survey my integration of other schools of psychoanalytic thought into my Jungian foundation, especially the work of Wilfred Bion and other post-Bionians. Additionally, I discuss general elements of the analytic experience that I emphasize in my practice.

Because of the intentionally brief nature of this introductory text on contemporary Jungian psychoanalysis, I was unable to include many clinical examples of the core concepts being discussed. From my perspective, this is an unfortunate consequence of brevity because my interest has always been in and my emphasis on the clinical application of psychoanalysis. This is the main concession made during the writing of this volume. This volume differs from other introductory texts on Jungian psychoanalysis in several ways. Most introductions to Jungian psychoanalysis are directed towards individuals with limited knowledge of other schools of psychoanalytic thought. Therefore, little effort is made to link Jungian concepts and practices with other psychoanalytic ideas and methods. Also, introductory Jungian texts are often oriented towards a broad general audience rather than practicing clinicians. This volume is specifically intended to introduce Jungian psychoanalysis to psychoanalysts and psychoanalytic psychotherapists who already possess a working knowledge of at least one other psychoanalytic orientation but have a limited exposure to the Jungian orientation. The second agenda for this volume is to provide a succinct overview of contemporary Jungian psychoanalysis, the debates occurring within analytical psychology, and the relationship between analytical psychology and psychoanalysis for those in training to become Jungian psychoanalysts or Jungian-oriented therapists. This volume provides a resource that touches on the essential foundational concepts and literature in Jungian psychoanalysis, as well as summarizing the contemporary debates occurring within analytical psychology. A similar volume has not appeared in the Jungian literature since Samuels' (1985) survey, *Jung and the Post-Jungians*, so the need for a new survey of the field was significant.

Ultimately, it is my hope that Jungian readers of this volume will see the value in linking Jungian ideas with concepts from other psychoanalytic perspectives. As Max Müller, one of the founders of the comparative study of religion, once said, "He who knows only one religion, knows none" (Stone 2016, p. xix). I believe the same holds true in psychoanalysis; having exposure to more than one theory of psychoanalysis refines our understanding of the primary system of psychoanalysis we are grounded in. In fact, Jung echoes a similar sentiment, "Ultimate truth … requires the concert of many voices" (1976, ¶1236). Jung even explicitly identifies himself as engaging analysis from a poly-theoretical perspective, "To my mind, in dealing with individuals, only individual understanding will do. We need a different language for every patient. In one analysis I can be heard talking the Adlerian dialect, in another the Freudian" (1965, p. 131). The aim of this volume is to introduce Jungian psychoanalysis to those less familiar with Jung's work and to continue seeking the "concert of many voices."

Notes

1 Past-President of the American Psychoanalytic Association and the International Psychoanalytical Association.
2 Referred to initially as the 'London school' in contrast to those who received their training within the 'Zurich school'.

Chapter 1

A Brief History of Analytical Psychology

The history of analytical psychology is intimately interwoven with Jung's relationship with Freud. Jung graduated as a physician from the University of Basel in 1900 and was appointed as an assistant psychiatrist under Eugen Bleuler at the Burghölzli Psychiatric Hospital in Zurich. During that time, he was influenced by the work of Freud and Josef Breuer, which had been published as *Studies in Hysteria* (1895/2004), as well as by the French neurologists Jean-Martin Charcot and Pierre Janet who were studying and treating dissociative disorders.

Jung attempted to read Freud's *Interpretation of Dreams* (1899/1955) shortly after its publication, but as a twenty-five-year-old newly minted psychiatrist, he felt he didn't have sufficient experience to grasp the implications of Freud's theories. Upon rereading it in 1903 Jung realized the empirical studies he was doing with the word association experiment (see Jung 1973a) supported Freud's theories, particularly Freud's theory of repression. In 1906 he initiated correspondence with Freud[1] and included a copy of his manuscript *Diagnostische Assoziationsstudien* (in Jung 1973b). Freud responded enthusiastically, excited to encounter a young research psychiatrist from a prominent psychiatric facility in Switzerland who was offering empirical support for his psychoanalytic theories. Freud was also excited to receive support from a non-Jew because he was concerned about the impact of anti-Semitism on the acceptance of psychoanalysis, already having to address characterizations of psychoanalysis as the "Jewish science" and reportedly telling his Jewish colleagues "Jung will save

DOI: 10.4324/9781003223511-2

us" (Johansson and Punzi 2019, p. 140). Freud responded on April 11, 1906, "Of course your latest paper, 'Psychoanalysis and Association Experiments' pleased me most, because in it you argue on the strength of your own experience that everything I have said about the hitherto unexplored fields of our discipline is true" (McGuire 1974, p. 3). Freud invited Jung to visit him in Vienna in 1907. They conversed for twelve hours uninterrupted during their first meeting, which reflects the intensity of their developing relationship often described as an intense, mutually idealizing father–son dynamic.

However, these initial exchanges were not without ambivalence for Jung who already was feeling pressure from Freud to support his theories with absolute fidelity. During one of their early exchanges, Jung recalls Freud imploring him, "My dear Jung, promise me never to abandon the sexual theory. That is the most essential thing of all. You see, we must make a dogma of it, an unshakable bulwark" (Jung 1965, p. 150). However, their relationship continued to unfold in a generally positive fashion, at least on the surface.

In 1909, both Freud and Jung were invited to lecture in the United States at Clark University in Worcester, Massachusetts. Freud also invited Sandor Ferenczi to accompany them. The men were together daily for seven weeks including the travel aboard ship. They analyzed one another's dreams regularly, but Freud refused to provide associations to some of his dreams and at one point fainted during a discussion of some mummified pre-historic bodies recently discovered in the peat bogs near Bremen, Germany – their city of embarkation.

Despite the underlying tensions that were beginning to emerge, Freud continued to promote Jung as his heir apparent in the psychoanalytic world. In 1910, with Freud's support, Jung was elected as the first president of the International Psychoanalytical Association (IPA) and appointed as the editor of the first journal devoted exclusively to psychoanalysis, the *Jahrbuch für psycho-analytische und psychopathologische Forschungen*. In the four short years following his initial contact with Freud, Jung had risen to the pinnacle of the psychoanalytic world, second only in stature to Freud.

However, Jung's concern about Freud's narrow interpretation of libido, i.e., as being primarily sexual in orientation, continued to distress Jung. He felt that the unconscious was not exclusively a repository of repressed wishes and impulses, but also included creative and spiritual impulses as well. Jung conceptualized libido as a broader life force that is experienced under a wide variety of experiences, in addition to sexuality. Jung introduced an alternative name for libido, namely 'psychic energy,' in an effort to convey the broader scope of libidinal energy. He also began to formulate ideas about a layer of the unconscious, which was not entirely personal and contained archaic vestiges of our species, i.e., a collective layer which Jung eventually named the collective unconscious, and he came to refer to its component structuring elements as archetypes. Jung published his ideas in 1912 in *Psychology of the Unconscious* (German: *Wandlungen und Symbole der Libido*) (Jung 1912/1991). This work was eventually revised and retitled as *Symbols of Transformation* (Jung 1956) when it was incorporated into Jung's *Collected Works*.

Jung recognized that the publication of views not fully consistent with Freud's conceptual model was going to alienate and create conflict with Freud. In the letters exchanged with Freud, Jung became more overtly critical and conflictual. Freud and his closest supporters commenced efforts to discredit Jung and his ideas, hoping they would force Jung to resign as president of the IPA. Jung came to recognize that he could not develop his ideas while remaining in the IPA and serving as president of the organization. In 1913 he resigned from the IPA and from his position as editor of the *Jahrbuch*.

Jung's break from Freud and the psychoanalytic community impacted Jung profoundly. It was a loss of professional position and identity, as well as a loss of his relationship with one of the most influential figures in his life. Although he continued seeing his analysands, he withdrew from many other areas of life. He experienced a great deal of uncertainty about his future path and was in a state of significant internal crisis. During this time of turning inward, from 1913–1916, which Ellenberger (1970) describes as a form of "creative illness," Jung underwent a period of personal self-exploration which consisted of imaginal dialogues with inner figures as well as painting images from those encounters. It was through this prolonged period of self-exploration that Jung hoped to discover and live into his personal myth. He initially recorded these internal dialogues in black notebooks which he called the *Black Books* (Jung 2020). From 1915 through 1930, Jung worked on extracting, shaping, and refining the content of the *Black Books* into the more focused work which ultimately became *The Red Book: Liber Novus* (Jung 2009).

As Jung emerged from his crisis, he entered the most prolific phase of his professional life. From 1915–1943 Jung laid out the conceptual and clinical foundations of analytical psychology: psychic energy (libido), the structure of the psyche (i.e., complexes, archetypes, instincts, and Self),[2] and his theory of consciousness. He also proposed that there is a transcendent characteristic of the unconscious (the collective unconscious), formulated an explanation for the movement of psychic energy based on a psychological tension of opposites, a theory of consciousness (i.e., typology), developed a new approach to dream analysis, and proposed a life-long process of psycho-spiritual development which he termed individuation. Knox summarizes these developments as follows:

> The key concepts that define the legacy from Jung that analytical psychologists strive to preserve include: 1) the self as an organizing psychic structure, 2) archetypes and the collective unconscious, 3) the dissociative nature of the psyche and the formation of complexes, 4) the unconscious as an active and purposive agent in individuation, 5) the psyche as self-regulating – the transcendent function, 6) libido as neutral psychic energy, available for a number of purposes, 7) psychic imagery as symbols not signs, reflecting something as yet unknown.
>
> (2007, p. 319)

A fuller exploration of these concepts will be developed in later chapters.

Jung suffered heart attacks in 1944 and 1946. From 1944 until his death in 1961, the focus of his work shifted. He continued to write about the clinical and conceptual ideas associated with analytical psychology, but the conceptual framework of analytical psychology was well established at this point, and Jung's primary focus shifted towards the exploration and articulation of archetypal and cultural themes – e.g., *The Philosophical Tree* (1945/1954), *Flying Saucers: A Modern Myth* (1950), *Answer to Job* (1952b), *Mysterium Coniunctionis* (1956/1963), and *Aion* (1959). However, a significant theme running through Jung's writing, from 1913 through to his death in 1961, was his ongoing agenda to differentiate his views from Freud's, while also giving credit to Freud where he felt it was due. For example, in Jung's last published book *Mysterium Coniunctionis* (1956/1963), which he considered to be his *magnum opus*, there are a number of references to Freud. Also, in his autobiography, there is a significant chapter describing his relationship with Freud (Jung 1965).

Like psychoanalysis as a whole, analytical psychology evolved during Jung's life and following his death. Samuels (1985, pp. 1–22) laid out a classification model to describe the various orientations within analytical psychology: i.e., classical, developmental, and archetypal. Samuels utilizes differing areas of clinical and theoretical emphasis to distinguish between these orientations. Since the publication of Samuels' book, a fourth model has emerged around the work of Wolfgang Giegerich. The students and adherents of Giegerich's ideas, sometimes referred to as 'Giegerichians,' have organized the International Society for Psychology as the Discipline of Interiority to further the development of Giegerich's orientation.

The classical model, originally referred to as the 'Zurich school,' follows closely the model laid out by Jung in his twenty-volume *Collected Works* (and in various supplemental volumes). In addition to those works, emphasis is also placed on the works of Marie-Louise von Franz, Erich Neumann, Emma Jung, and Edward Edinger (among others) – all authors who hold closely to Jung's original lines of thought. Analysts associated with the Zurich school did not necessarily live in Zurich, although many had attended seminars there or had done some of their personal analysis there. Originally, there was no formal training program in Zurich and Jung was initially resistant to the idea of forming a training institute around his model. Instead, there was an ongoing series of seminars by Jung and his close collaborators sponsored by the Zurich Psychology Club which was founded in 1916. The classical school places greater emphasis on the concept and function of the Self and on the exploration of archetypal themes emerging in analysis, with comparatively less emphasis on childhood developmental experiences, the analysis of defenses, or the analysis of the transference–countertransference relationship.

The developmental orientation was originally referred to as the 'London school' (in contrast to the 'Zurich school') which originated in London in the 1940s under the influence of Michael Fordham and the Society for Analytical Psychology (SAP). Fordham was a psychiatrist and Jungian psychoanalyst who treated children, adolescents, adults. He was one of the first Jungian analysts to openly question elements of Jung's conceptual framework and to offer revisions of Jung's theories.

The first formal Jungian training program was established by the SAP in 1946.[3] Uneasy with the idealizations that had grown up around Jung, Fordham said in his autobiography, "It was … because I held that we were serving a science, that I insisted on calling our society the Society of Analytical Psychology and not the C.G. Jung Institute" (Fordham 1993, p. 94). Fordham and the SAP were strongly influenced by the work of Melanie Klein and object relations theorists such as Donald Winnicott, Ronald Fairbairn, and Harry Guntrip. Fordham felt the classical Jungian approach was not well suited to all patients and that there were deficits in the model of Jungian training prior to the founding of the SAP:

> Training in Jung's methods of dream analysis and the use of active imagination were clear enough. But that meant acquiring considerable knowledge of myth, legend and religious practices so that amplification could be used. There was no analyst who was able to do enough of that. Jung's publications of psychotherapy included, it is true, the application of psychoanalysis and Adlerian psychology to suitable cases as indicated by Jung's type system, but that was not much used. That may seem quite a comprehensive program when combined, as it was, with the analysis of the candidate, but the methods used by Jung, and more so by his followers, were not applicable

often in the rough and tumble of everyday psychotherapy when the careful analysis of sexuality and childhood was often needed but neglected.

(Fordham 1998, p. 56)

Elsewhere, Fordham indicated,

I needed the knowledge which psychoanalysts had accumulated, owing to insufficient work having been done on childhood by Jungians – a defect that I was attempting to rectify. However, many Jungians felt that what I thought of, and acknowledged, as necessary criticism of Jungian thought and practices was destructive of Jungian theories and practices.

(1993, p. 137)

Clearly, Fordham's incorporation of psychoanalytic ideas and techniques into Jung's model was not received well by those aligned with the Zurich model. This tension eventually led to the first split within the Jungian community in London – with adherents of the 'Zurich' model, led by Gerhard Adler, splitting off in 1976 to form the Association of Jungian Analysts (AJA).

The developmental school places more emphasis on the developmental history of the patient, a closer weaving of the personal with the archetypal dimensions of experience, the analysis of defenses, and the analysis of the transference–countertransference matrix (Fordham 1978, Siegelman 1994). Additionally, the SAP has incorporated infant observation training as part of their curriculum for all candidates in both the adult and the child/adolescent tracks of their training program.

The developmental school is the group within analytical psychology that has been the most open to the cross-pollination of ideas from other fields of study, e.g., somatic research and embodiment (Dunlea 2019), infant research (Jacoby 1999), attachment theory, emergence theory, systems theory, and neuroscience (Wilkinson 2006, 2010; Knox 2003, 2011), as well as influences from other models of psychoanalysis, such as the work of Harold Searles (Sedgewick 1993), Robert Langs (White 2023), Heinz Kohut and self-psychology (Jacoby 1984, 1990; Schwartz-Salant

1982), Wilfred Bion (Culbert-Koehn 1997, 2000; Sullivan 2010; Winborn 2018), Ignacio Matte Blanco (Carvalho 2014; Corbett 2020), relational psychoanalysis (Sedgwick 2012; Colman 2013; West 2017), and intersubjectivity (Colman 2007; Cwik 2017; Maier 2014; Schwartz-Salant 1995).

The archetypal school emerged from the work of James Hillman in the 1970s. Like the developmental school, Hillman also perceived the classical Jungian approach as lacking or misguided in certain aspects, but his emphasis was on quite different areas of focus than those of the developmental school. Hillman was particularly critical of Jung's conceptualization of the psyche as revolving around an overarching, central organizing principle which Jung termed the Self. Hillman argued that Jung's concept of Self paralleled the rise of monotheism in world religions which led to the demise or suppression of most polytheistic religions – such as the Greek pantheon of gods and goddesses. This was problematic for Hillman who proposed that the psyche functions in a polytheistic manner, reflecting a multiplicity of centers. From Hillman's polytheistic perspective, it is desirable not to be integrated and centered, but to be flexible, embracing, shifting, and complex. According to Hillman, "Polytheistic psychology obliges consciousness to circulate among a field of powers. Each god has his due as each complex deserves its respect in its own right" (Hillman 1989, p. 40).

Hillman argued that the fundamental experience of the psyche was accessed through images, particularly dream images, hence his rule of thumb "stick to the image" (Hillman 1983). Hillman says,

> When an image is realized – fully imagined as a living being other than myself – then it becomes a *psychopompos*, a guide with a soul having its own inherent limitation and necessity. It is this image and no other, so that the conceptual questions of moral pluralism and relativism fade in front of the actual engagement of the image.
>
> (1989, p. 56)

While the concept of archetypes is central to archetypal psychology, from Hillman's perspective the archetype does not to connect the individual to a transcendent element of experience, but rather serves as a background generator of images. What Hillman meant by this was that we should avoid translating images into meanings, particularly the translation of images into psychological theories or attempting to move the individual's experience of their image towards a broader interpretation of the image within the context of a myth, fairy tale, religion, or alchemical process.

Hillman argued that the ever-deepening experience of an image was what brought us into closer contact with 'soul' and therefore was 'soul-making,' not the translation of image into some other language or metaphor. However, for Hillman soul-making occurred 'in the world' rather than into some transcendent or redemptive realm beyond the world. Quoting the poet Wallace Stevens, he said "The way through the world is more difficult to find than the way beyond it" (1989, p. 26). Hillman felt that the central question of soul-making is "what does this event, this thing, this moment move in my soul?" (1989, p. 27). He also indicated, "The dream is thus making soul each night" (1989, p. 28).

For Hillman, imagining is the central act of engagement with images. Hillman indicates, "The thought of the heart is the thought of images, the heart is the seat of the imagination, the imagination is the authentic voice of the heart, so if we speak from the heart we must speak imaginatively" (1981, p. 2). Hillman juxtaposes the term 'soul' with 'spirit.' He argued that psychology had become too infused with agendas from the scientific, spiritual, and philosophical fields – therefore becoming too spiritualized, too closely associated with the fixed ideas, too detached, and too invested in the position of objective observer. Hillman felt contemporary psychology no longer embraced soul which he associated more with Eros and a poetic basis of the psyche.

Hillman's orientation to psychopathology also incorporates his emphasis on the image-making aspect of soul. Taking up a quote from Jung, "The Gods have become our diseases," Hillman proposes that our pathologies, our symptoms, our neuroses are a way of mythmaking (1980, p. 2). He indicates,

I would like to extend our concept of psychopathology by introducing the term pathologizing by which I mean: the psyche's autonomous ability to create illness, morbidity, disorder, abnormality, and suffering in any aspect of its behavior, and to experience and imagine life through this deformed and afflicted perspective.

(1980, p. 1)

Elsewhere, he says, "Only in mythology does pathology receive an adequate mirror, since myths speak with the same distorted, fantastic language [as our pathologies]" (1989, p. 146).

Clearly, Hillman's emphasis, as well as others writing and practicing analysis from this perspective, is not on extending psychological conceptualization or the application of specific clinical techniques. The emphasis of the archetypal school is on cultivating a philosophy, attitude, or ethos; an aesthetic-poetic sensibility that informs how the analyst engages with a patient and seeks a broad, non-specific outcome from the analytic process – i.e., that of engaging imagination and soul-making.

As mentioned earlier, since the publication of Samuels' (1985) classification system for the various schools or orientations associated with analytical psychology, a fourth school has emerged around Wolfgang Giegerich. Giegerich is a Jungian analyst who was initially aligned with the archetypal school. However, he came to believe that Hillman and his followers did not go far enough in their critique of Jung's concepts and approach to the psyche. Giegerich's writing mainly focuses on identifying the philosophical/logical flaws and limitations in the theories of Jung, while offering is own reinterpretation of Jung's concepts. Much of Giegerich's critique is formulated around the philosophical ideas of Hegel and Heidegger. In general, Giegerich argues that Jung and Jungians are not sufficiently critical of the concepts they utilize.

Because any psychology is inherently subjective, Giegerich proposes that the concepts, theories, and practices associated with that psychology are an expression of the psyche they were developed to explain. Therefore, the discipline of psychology must be a self-critical, self-reflective one and it must abandon any claim to objectivity or having objective knowledge. Furthermore, Giegerich argues that psychology is inherently subjective because it is embedded within the historical-cultural context that it arises from. He also argues that psychology must not satisfy itself only with the imaginal life of the soul because the soul also has a logical life. He indicates that soul doesn't just imagine and fantasize, it also does think and has a need to think.

Like Hillman and others associated with the archetypal school, the term 'soul' appears frequently in Giegerich's writing and in the titles of his books, such as *The Soul's Logical Life* (1998), *Soul-Violence* (2008), *The Soul Always Thinks* (2010), and *What is Soul?* (2012). Giegerich is critical of Hillman's way of depicting soul and soul-making. According to Giegerich, Hillman reduces soul-making to the poetic and metaphorical. He goes on to claim this is a benign version of the notion of soul-making which fails to recognize the true nature of soul. In Giegerich's writing, 'the soul' does not have a fixed meaning. It is the byproduct of ongoing objective thought or logical life, which Giegerich calls *mindedness*. His emphasis here is on the lack of a substantiated soul as a separate producing agent behind psychic phenomena. For Giegerich, soul is an ongoing production, not a thing or a personification. Giegerich argues there is only the actually occurring logical life or thinking itself with no literal embodied soul behind it.

In addition to his focus on 'soul,' Giegerich constructs a vocabulary for his school of thought, including concepts such as interiority, truth, rationality, logic, negation, sublation, and syzygy. Often, he defines and utilizes these concepts differently than they are used in psychology, philosophy, or analytical psychology. As with authors from the archetypal school, it can be difficult to discern the direct application of Giegerich's conceptual framework in the consulting room. Interestingly, Giegerich says his writing has little to do with the consulting room, other than preparing the analyst's mind to do analytic work,

> I make a strict difference between psychological theory and work in the consulting room. The former serves to my mind the sole purpose of training the mind, educating the mind: teaching it to think psychologically and becoming able to really take a psychological standpoint. It does not have the

purpose of establishing a theory to be applied to the work with patients. In the consulting room I try to be present with such a psychologically-trained consciousness, but otherwise forget theories and approach the patient unprejudiced (as much as is humanly possible) in the spirit of *Nowness* and *Eachness*. The concentration is on this phenomenon now. … And the question is: what does it need?

(quoted in Casement 2011, p. 539)

In summary, analytical psychology has evolved in significantly different directions over the 110 years since Jung published *Psychology of the Unconscious* in 1912, just as psychoanalysis has evolved, splintered, and subjected the original contributions of Freud to critical re-evaluation. While analytical psychology was born out of the differences, both theoretical and personal, between Jung and Freud, I believe there is the possibility of greater rapprochement and cross-fertilization between analytical psychology and other schools of psychoanalytic thought, i.e., to identify and build from "the common ground of psychoanalysis" (Wallerstein 1992).

Notes

1 Correspondence which continued until 1913 (see McGuire 1974).
2 Jung did not capitalize the term 'self' in his writings. However, it has become commonplace in Jungian literature to present 'self' in its capitalized form 'Self.' This convention will generally be utilized throughout this volume. The primary function of this practice is to make a distinction between the use of 'self' in ordinary daily language and to distinguish Jung's use of the term from other psychoanalytic authors, e.g., Winnicott, Kohut, Kernberg, Khan, and Jacobson. The capitalized 'Self' is specifically used to designate the primary organizing structure of the individual psyche but also to convey Jung's conceptualization of the Self as possessing a transcendent aspect which is connected with something beyond the personal psyche, which Jung often refers to as 'the God-image.' See Gordon (1985) for a fuller description of the use of 'self' in analytical psychology and other psychoanalytic models.
3 Followed by the establishment of the C.G. Jung Institute in Zurich/ Küsnacht in 1948.

Suggestions for Further Reading

General

Astor, J. (2002). Analytical psychology and its relation to psychoanalysis:
   A personal view. *J. Anal. Psych., 47*: 599–612.
Eisold, K. (2002). Jung, Jungians, and psychoanalysis. *Psychoanal. Psychol., 19* (*3*): 501–524.
Kirsch, T. (2000). *The Jungians: A Comparative and Historical Perspective*. London: Routledge.
Samuels, A. (1985). *Jung and the Post-Jungians*. London: Routledge.

Developmental School

Astor, J. (1995). *Michael Fordham: Innovations in Analytical Psychology*.
   London: Routledge.

Archetypal School

Hillman, J. (1983). *Archetypal Psychology: A Brief Account*. Dallas, TX:
   Spring Publications.

Giegerich

Giegerich, W. (2005). *The Collected English Papers, Vol. 1: The Neurosis
   of Psychology: Primary Papers toward a Critical Psychology*. New
   Orleans: Spring Journal Books.

Chapter 2

Aims and Attitudes in Jungian Psychoanalysis

In terms of aims, a traditional perspective in psychoanalysis is that the only aim of the psychoanalytic process is doing the work of analyzing. However, as Sandler and Dreher (1996) argue, all psychoanalysts carry aims and attitudes, whether implicitly or explicitly, influenced by the theoretical orientations they have been exposed to and the identifications they have formed with various figures in their training and development as psychoanalysts.

Most psychoanalytic orientations hold several characteristics in common, although the conceptual understanding of these characteristics may differ, e.g.: 1) the thoughts, feelings, behaviors, and self-image of individuals are often influenced by unconscious factors; 2) psychoanalytic treatment explores how these unconscious factors affect current relationships; 3) the analytic process traces these patterns back to their historical origins, considering how these patterns have evolved over time, thereby allowing the individual to cope better with the realities of their current life situation; 4) by working through internal obstacles to change (i.e., defense mechanisms), analysis aims at freeing the patient to make less emotionally restricted choices in life; 5) analytic therapy takes place in the context of an intimate partnership, in the course of which the patient becomes aware of the underlying sources, not simply intellectually but emotionally as well, in part by re-experiencing them with the analyst; and 6) the patient and analyst work together to establish a safe and trusting relationship that enables the patient to experience aspects of his or her inner life that have been hidden because they are painful, embarrassing, disavowed, or guilt-provoking.

DOI: 10.4324/9781003223511-3

Most contemporary Jungian analysis and therapists would likely endorse these characteristics of analysis, however, there would be several additional characteristics which Jungians would add to these general characteristics, i.e.: 1) analytical psychology endeavors to discern the influence of the collective or universal elements of the psyche (i.e., *archetypes* and *instincts*) on the life of the individual; 2) in addition to historical origins, analytical psychologists attempt to discern how the psyche is moving towards or anticipating the future of the individual (i.e., *teleological* or *prospective* aspect of psyche); and 3) a process associated with the ultimate goal of Jungian analysis, i.e., *individuation* (a coming into the wholeness of one's own being).

Teleology

Teleology is the explanation of phenomena by the purpose they serve rather than through the identification of the causes of the phenomena. In other words, a teleological perspective asks what purpose a psychic phenomenon serves and where it is moving to. The teleological thrust in Jung is strongly represented in his concept of the transcendent function (Jung 1958) which Jung proposes as the internal mechanism by which opposites of psychological experience are transformed via a higher synthesis into a new third quality of experience.

As Alvarez (1992, p. 175) says, "The prospective, forward-looking and aspiring element in human nature has always been important in Jungian analytic theory." Similarly, Jung uses to the term transcendence to refer to levels of experience which move beyond the personal and solely subjective. Jung uses a variety of terms to address this level of experience; 'archetypal,' 'collective unconscious,' 'objective psyche,' and 'Self.' Similarly, Grotstein notes the parallel between Jung and Bion in terms of the teleological thrust of the psyche,

> I think they both [Jung and Bion] were going in the same direction, in a kind of poetic language which indicated what we see and know is limited by our senses. There is a coherence beyond. I think that's one of the principal things that unites

Jung with Bion, that there is something beyond, before, and in the future.

(Grotstein in Culbert-Koehn 1997, p. 18)

Individuation

The teleological element in Jung's model is most fully developed in his concept of individuation which Jung saw as the ultimate goal of the analytic process. Individuation refers to an ongoing, progressive process of coming into the fullness of one's own being. Jung defines individuation as, "becoming an 'in-dividual,' and, in so far as 'individuality' embraces our innermost, last, and incomparable uniqueness, it also implies becoming one's own self. We could therefore translate individuation as 'coming to selfhood' or 'self-realization'" (1966, ¶266). He also conceptualizes individuation as the process by which the Self is synthesized with the rest of the personality, "The goal of the individuation process is the synthesis of the self" (1969, ¶278).

Jung sees individuation as being a process rooted in our instincts, "The dynamic of this process is instinct, which ensures that everything which belongs to an individual's life shall enter into it" (1952b, ¶745). While Jung saw individuation as a naturally occurring process, whether experienced unconsciously or consciously, he conceived of it as a process of maturation that was deepened and accelerated by the analytic process (Jung 1969, ¶270). Jung also saw the process of individuation as a process which becomes more prominent or consciously engaged during the second half of life, after leaving the parental home and establishing one's family, occupational identity, and some degree of financial stability, i.e., tasks typically undertaken during the first half of life which Jung referred to collectively as the hero's journey.

Upon entering the second half of life, Jung observed there was often a diminishment or loss of meaning in these extraverted life accomplishments which also frequently resulted in some form of malaise, depression, or anxiety. Jung referred to the onset of these symptoms as the neuroses of the second half of life (Jung 1977, p. 108) but he also referred to this life phase through various archetypal themes, e.g., 'the dark night of the soul,' 'the night sea journey,' or the *Nekyia* (an ancient Greek cult-practice in which the dead are consulted about the future). Jung saw this phase as an introversion of focus necessary for the individuation process, e.g., "The Nekyia is no aimless or destructive fall into the abyss, but a meaningful *katabasis* [descent into the lower world] ... its object the restoration of the whole man" (1934, ¶213).

Many Jungian analysts continue to view individuation as a process primarily occurring during the second half of life. However, beginning in 1944, Michael Fordham proposed a revision of Jung's model of individuation (Fordham 1994). Fordham was a Jungian psychoanalyst and psychiatrist who treated children and adolescents before, during, and after World War II. Much later in his career he also undertook the infant observation training at the Tavistock Clinic in London. Through his work with children and adolescents, Fordham was convinced that the Self was an active factor in shaping development throughout the life span, from birth onward. He proposed that there was a 'primary self' present from birth that requires the presence of primary caregivers to facilitate the 'unpacking' and metabolizing of the potential elements contained in the infant's nascent self so that they can be reintegrated as active components of the infant's self-structure. Fordham referred to this as the deintegrate–integrate process (Fordham 1971). Fordham's perspective on the existence of a primary self in infants and the interactive nature of the emergence and development of the self-structure is now strongly supported by contemporary developmental research, such as Stern (1985) and Beebe and Lachmann (2002).

Consciousness

A key focus in Jungian analysis and the individuation process is the development of consciousness. Jung defines consciousness as "the function of activity which maintains the relationship of psychic contents to the ego" (Jung 1971, ¶700). Consciousness is intimately connected with the capacity to form discriminate one's experience, "the whole essence of consciousness is discrimination, distinguishing ego from non-ego, subject from object, positive from negative. ... The separation into pairs of opposites is entirely due to conscious differentiation ... where no consciousness exists ... there is no reflection" (Jung 1971, ¶179). Therefore, Jungian psychoanalysis emphasizes the expansion of consciousness as a byproduct and goal of analysis with the assumption that consciousness will shift from ego centeredness towards a point of view more consistent with the totality of the personality (i.e., the Self). Analytical psychology uses insight as a tool for increasing consciousness. The central role of consciousness to Jungian psychoanalysis is summarized by Edinger as follows, "The purpose of human life is the creation of consciousness" (1984, p. 57, paraphrasing Jung 1965, p. 326).

While consciousness, especially as it relates to unconscious processes, is certainly an important aspect of Jungian psychoanalysis, the dichotomization of experience into only conscious and unconscious elements does not account for newer developments in psychoanalytic theory, such as the work of the Boston Change Process Study Group (Stern et al. 1998) who describe three levels of experience that influence the analytic process: 1) unconscious process, 2) conscious processes which BCPSG refer to as the explicit domain, and 3) the implicit domain which BCPSG define as experiences which are not in conscious awareness but are not dynamically held out of awareness by defense processes.

Bion also has a somewhat different perspective on the relationship between consciousness and unconscious process. Bion's model is not focused on increasing consciousness or making the unconscious conscious. His model focuses on the emergence of the experience of being, and dreaming is conceptualized as occurring in the background of experience, whether in a sleeping state or waking. Thought of this way, dream experience (waking or nocturnal) is not a process of making unconscious contents conscious. Rather it is a means of soaking consciousness in the stream of unconsciousness. Bion's model depicts a fluid, paradoxical relationship between unconscious and conscious experience. Therefore, it can be seen as a conceptualization of dreaming which moves back and forth between consciousness and unconsciousness. It reflects the indeterminate nature of dreaming and openness we must entertain/tolerate in relationship to dream material – both waking and nocturnal (Grotstein 2007).

Symbolic Attitude and Reflective Function

In Jungian psychoanalysis, the development of the symbolic attitude and the reflective function are closely connected with the
development of consciousness. The symbolic attitude is the phrase
Jung uses to describe someone with the capacity for symbolic
process:

> The attitude that takes a given phenomenon as symbolic may be
> called … the *symbolic attitude*. It is only partially justified by the
> behaviour of things; for the rest, it is the outcome of a definite
> view of the world which assigns meaning to events, and attaches
> to this meaning a greater value than to bare facts.
>
> (1971, ¶819)

The symbolic attitude will be addressed more fully in Chapter 6 in
the section on symbols. It can be considered a subset of the
broader concept of the analytic attitude (Winborn 2019).

Jung (1960/1969, ¶246) also hypothesizes the existence of a
reflective instinct, that is, the tendency to search for meaning and
to reflect on experience, as one of five primary instincts for all
human beings. The capacity for reflection is a necessary component in the development of symbolic capacity. Fonagy (2000) and
others use the terms 'mentalization' and 'reflective function' interchangeably to refer to the patient's capacity to reflect upon,
understand, and make inferences about one's own experience and
motivations, as well as the experience and motivations of others.
Or to put it more simply, the capacity to "think about thinking"
(Fonagy 1991).

Similarly, Bion (1962/1983), in his model of the psyche, proposes a
theory of thinking which focuses on the individual's capacity to digest
experience, not only the capacity for reflection about experience but
the capacity for the mental representation of experience as well. Bion
refers frequently to 'thinking' in his writing, but his concept of thinking is not synonymous with cognition or intellectual acts. He uses the
term 'thinking' as a shorthand for the capacity *for being* through the
reflective, embodied experiencing of emotion. Hence, the capacity
to process emotional experience is the foundation from which

increasingly complex forms of reflection emerge, such as Jung's concept of the symbolic attitude. Hence, increased capacity in consciousness, the reflective function, and the symbolic attitude can all be considered desired outcomes of Jungian psychoanalysis.

The Unknown

An embrace of the unknown or mysterious element in psychological experience also features prominently in Jung's concept of the engagement with the unconscious:

> The unconscious is not simply the unknown, it is rather the unknown psychic; and this we define on the one hand as all those things in us which, if they came to consciousness, would presumably differ in no respect from the known psychic contents, with the addition … of the psychoid system, of which nothing is known directly.
>
> (1960/1969, ¶382)

This element is also reflected in Bion's model of the psyche with his emphasis on what he terms "negative capability" (Bion 1970/1983). Negative capability is a term Bion borrowed from the British poet John Keats who used it in a letter to his brothers. In that letter, Keats defined negative capability as the capacity to embrace uncertainty, live with mystery, and make peace with ambiguity, without an insistence that unconscious factors conform with fact and reason.

Analytic Aims and the Reconciliation of Analytical Psychology and Psychoanalysis

Two primary themes have emerged in psychoanalysis which set the stage for a closer dialogue between psychoanalysis and analytical psychology: 1) a greater openness to psycho-spiritual themes in the analytic encounter (Gordon 2004; Tennes 2007; Rosegrant 2012), and 2) increased interest in the creative and generative aspects of the unconscious (Newirth 2003; Safran 2006). The transpersonal, generative, and creative aspects of the unconscious are all central to Jung's model of psychic functioning and serve as a conceptual bridge for those in the psychoanalytic community moving towards rapprochement with Jung.

Gordon (2004) draws on the work of Wilfred Bion, Donald Winnicott, Christopher Bollas, James Grotstein, and Michael Eigen, as well as some influences from relational psychoanalysis, to support his call for the restoration of wonderment and the experience of numinosity (Otto 1923/1965) to the psychoanalytic dialogue. As Gordon puts it:

> There is a basic human tendency to seek experience of the numinous. … We are presupposed in this way. Relatively recently … these efforts have been largely disconnected from their original wonderment and replaced with primarily rational or practical intentions. And the results have been devastating. With the removal of numinous experience from everyday life, a central dimension of self-experience has been flattened, its potential richness desiccated. … In the extreme, this gives rise to the feelings of emptiness and purposelessness that are the background canvas of so many of our patients' lives, no matter the particulars that first bring them to treatment.
>
> (2004, p. 6)

Later, Gordon (2004, p. 7) succinctly states, "There also seems to be a concomitant universal psychic imperative: to seek experience that connects us, temporarily but repeatedly, with the transcendent."

Similarly, Tennes (2007) points out that psychoanalytic theory has avoided embracing the mysterious and the unknowable, particularly in the analytic encounter. Like Gordon, she also references Bion, Eigen, Grotstein, and Bollas as the primary psychoanalytic authors who have incorporated the ineffable unknown as a centerpiece in their analytic frameworks. Tennes proposes that psychoanalysis as a field is on the verge of a paradigm shift: a move towards greater openness to spiritual dimensions of experience. Her discussion centers on the 'transpersonal' aspects of experience which point beyond intersubjective dimensions of experience to an encounter with "ontological otherness" (2007, p. 515). Bion's concept of 'O' (similar in description to Jung's concept of Self and the objective elements of the psyche, i.e., the archetypes) is the psychoanalytic concept Tennes highlights as best expressing the ontological otherness that serves as an objective ground of being, informing our individual subjectivity. In the context of this discussion, she states:

> The theory and practice of Jungian analysis is without doubt the approach that most extensively explores the integration of spiritual realities into depth psychotherapy. … Because Jungian theory has tended to be overlooked within psychoanalytic circles, however, the spiritual dimension articulated there remains split off from psychoanalytic thought, however well developed it may be.
>
> (2007, p. 512, fn 4)

Rosegrant (2012), like Gordon and Tennes, also examines the emerging role of the transpersonal in psychoanalysis, but does so through the analytic theories of Jung and Bion. He points out that they both attend to a layer of experience beyond the personal, "a commitment for connecting with a higher truth outside of personal experience" (2012, p. 721). Newirth (2003) and Safran (2006) focus attention on the generative, creative aspects of the unconscious rather than the transpersonal. Safran indicates that:

> There has been a recent resurgence of interest in the unconscious by relational analysts, as exemplified in the work of such theorists as James Grotstein and Michael Eigen as well as some of Stephen Mitchell's later writing. But the picture of the unconscious that emerges from these authors is a different one from Freud's unconscious and from the writing of many European analysts. The unconscious that emerges in these writings is one that is creative and generative, rather than one that is dangerous or destructive. And the emphasis of these authors is on harnessing unconscious forces or being guided by them, rather than taming or modulating them.
>
> (Safran, 2006, p. 394)

The Analytic Relationship: The Mutual Influence of Patient and Analyst

Jung's conception of the analytic relationship was that it was mutually influential and interactive, often referring to it as a dialectical process (Beebe, Cambray, and Kirsch 2001). He states this in various ways throughout his writing, often drawing upon analogies from alchemical writing, e.g., "The meeting of two personalities is like the contact of two chemical substances: if there is any reaction, both are transformed" (Jung 1933, p. 49). Jung did not believe the process could be transformative unless the analyst was 'in' the process with the patient:

> In any thoroughgoing analysis the whole personality of both patient and doctor is called into play. There are many cases which the doctor cannot cure without committing himself. When important matters are at stake, it makes all the difference whether the doctor sees himself as a part of the drama, or cloaks himself in his authority.
>
> (1965, pp. 132–133)

Another statement of this perspective follows:

> For two personalities to meet is like mixing two different chemical substances: If there is any combination at all both are transformed. In any effective psychological treatment, the doctor is bound to influence the patient: But this influence can only take place if the patient has a reciprocal influence on the doctor. You can exert no influence if you are not susceptible to influence.
>
> (Jung 1954/1966, ¶163)

Jung depicted the reciprocal influence of the analyst and analysand schematically in Figure 2.1 (1946, ¶422). In this diagram Jung identifies the various levels or modes of interaction and influence between analyst and analysand, i.e., conscious to conscious, conscious to unconscious, and unconscious to unconscious.

Jung's conceptualization of the analytic dyad has been described as possessing characteristics which anticipated the relational (Sedgwick 2012; Colman 2013; West 2017) and intersubjective

Analytic Relationship

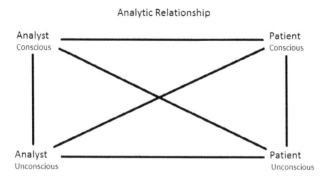

Figure 2.1 Jung's diagram of the analytic relationship.

(Colman 2007; Cwik 2017; Schwartz-Salant 1995) perspectives in psychoanalysis. Intersubjectivity theory (Atwood and Stolorow 1979) holds that psychoanalysis is an intersubjective experience, i.e., that there are two subjectivities present which create an interactive, mutually created psychological field in which elements of the individual psyches cannot be clearly distinguished (Ogden 1994). This contrasts with the traditional Freudian view of the analytic dyad as being composed of two distinct and isolated psyches, what intersubjectivists have come to term the myth of the isolated mind. Jung's theories on the nature of the analytic interaction can be seen as a precursory formulation of the fundamental tenets of intersubjectivity and relational psychoanalysis, just as Sandor Ferenczi's work has been described. A similar interactive perspective is also found in Bion's work:

In psycho-analysis: when approaching the unconscious – that is, what we do *not* know, not what we *do* know – we, patient and analyst alike, are certain to be disturbed. Anyone who is going to see a patient tomorrow should, at some point, experience fear. In every consulting room there ought to be two rather frightened people: the patient and the psycho-analyst. If they are not, one wonders why they are bothering to find out what everyone knows.

(Bion 1990, pp. 4–5)

Jung's fullest description of the mutual influence of the analytic relationship is found in his 1946 essay *The Psychology of the Transference* (Jung 1946).

Suggestions for Further Reading

Braun, C. (2020). *The Therapeutic Relationship in Analytical Psychology: Theory and Practice.* London: Routledge.

Carotenuto, A. (1992). *The Difficult Art: A Critical Discourse on Psychotherapy.* Wilmette, IL: Chiron.

Edinger, E. (1984). *The Creation of Consciousness: Jung's Myth for Modern Man.* Toronto: Inner City Books.

Sedgwick, D. (2001). *Introduction to Jungian Psychotherapy: The Therapeutic Relationship.* Brighton: Brunner-Routledge.

Chapter 3

Structure and Stratification of the Psyche

Archetypes and the Collective Unconscious

Jung's conceptualization of the structural components of the psyche is often the greatest hurdle for analysts and therapists from other schools of psychoanalysis to assimilate. It is important to note that Jung's direct engagement with Freud was during the time Freud was still working within his topographic model of the psyche. Freud's topographic model delineated the psyche into three domains – consciousness, preconscious, and unconscious. It was not until 1923 that Freud proposed a revised model of the psyche around three competing psychic agencies – id, ego, and superego – which came to be referred to as the structural model. Jung (1916/1928) modifies Freud's topographic model by eliminating Freud's idea of a preconscious and introducing a collective or impersonal element of the psyche: conscious, unconscious (deriving from personal experience), and collective unconscious (initially referred to as the 'impersonal unconscious'). Hence, a major disagreement between Jung and Freud was around Jung's proposal that there were innate, a priori elements of the psyche common to all humans which extended beyond personal experience.

Archetype

Based on imagery from his own dreams, the dreams of his patients, and the hallucinations of psychotic patients he was treating while a staff psychiatrist at the Burghölzli Psychiatric Hospital in Zurich, Jung noticed parallels with various motifs he found in ancient religious and mythological texts. Jung was

DOI: 10.4324/9781003223511-4

particularly struck by the parallel between a patient's vision of the Sun with a phallus moving back forth in the wind and a description found in the *Mithras Liturgy* (Dieterich 1910) which described wind emanating from a pipe or tube hanging from the Sun. Jung felt confident the patient could not have been familiar with the description because the text was not translated and published until several years after the patient described his vision to Jung. When Jung introduced the idea of impersonal elements of the unconscious, he initially referred to them as 'primordial ideas' (borrowing from Adolf Bastian) and only later adopted the term 'archetype,' a term which first appears in Jung's writings in 1919 (1960/1969, ¶270).

According to Jacobi (1973), the development of Jung's concept of the archetype was most influenced by St. Augustine's 'principal ideas,' but Jung also acknowledges being influenced by Lucien Lévy-Bruhl's concept of 'représentations collectives' (1936, ¶89). Jung has sometimes been referred to as a *bricoleur*, which describes someone who creates using whatever materials are available. In many respects, Jung's conceptual gift lay not in developing completely original ideas, but rather in gathering ideas from disparate sources while perceiving the intrinsic relationship between the various ideas and creating a system from this assemblage.

Solomon (1991, p. 313) provides a succinct summary of the concept of archetypes, "Archetypes are … thought of as unconscious universal structures, inherited blueprints, or templates, which organise psychic energy along certain repeatable and recognizable lines. These innate patterns or predispositions to the formation of typical ideas or behaviors become manifest through images, or symbols." Inherent in Solomon's summary is the idea that archetypes exist as potentials in everyone, serving to shape perception, feeling, ideas, and behaviors along certain paths. Hence, archetypes operate at the unconscious level but shape or influence conscious experience, i.e., "Archetypes intervene in the shaping of conscious contents by regulating, modifying and motivating them" (Jung 1960/1969, ¶404).

For example, one of Jung's early articulations of an archetypal motif is in a chapter from his 1912 volume *Psychology of the Unconscious* in a chapter titled, "The Unconscious Origin of the Hero" (1912/1991, ¶282–317) which outlines common characteristics of the hero motif from various religions and mythologies. Joseph Campbell (1949), in *Hero of a Thousand Faces*, articulated various elements of the hero motif that repeat across various hero stories through various mythologies and religions. Another example is provided by Neumann (1972), who writes about the Great Mother, the archetype which forms the universal background of experience to the personal mother. A specific archetypal image of the Great Mother would be Demeter, the mother of Persephone in Greek mythology.

An archetype provides underlying structure to experience but does not determine the specific presentation when it appears to consciousness as an image. Here, image is used loosely to describe a figure, process, object, or situation. In addition to the hero, other archetypal figures include father, mother, the ruler/leader/king/queen, the victim, villain, trickster, magician/sage, priest/prophet, healer, mystic, acolyte/initiate, hunter, and so on. Any role/figure that has general universality across generations and cultures can potentially be an archetype, but how that archetype manifests in different eras and cultures will vary. Processes such as journey, ascent, or descent can be considered archetypal. Places can also be archetypal, such as boundaries, crossroads, places of refuge, places of initiation, bridges, or entrances, gates, and doorways.

Archetypes can be thought of as functional and prefigurative potentials which move experience along certain paths. Speaking of archetypes, Jung indicates:

> These contents have one outstanding peculiarity, and that is their mythological character. It is as if they belong to a pattern not particular to any particular mind or person, but rather to a pattern peculiar to *mankind in general* … and therefore they are of a collective nature. These collective patterns I have called *archetypes*.
>
> (1935, ¶79–80, italics in original)

Relatively early in the development of the concept, Jung spoke of archetypes as inherited ideas:

> Archetypes are systems of readiness for action, and at the same time images and emotions. They are inherited with the

brain structure – indeed they are its psychic aspect. ... They are thus, essentially, the chthonic portion of the psyche ... that portion through which the psyche is attached to nature.

(1931a, ¶53)

Later, Jung modifies his position regarding the direct biological inheritance of archetypes, "It is not, therefore, a question ... of inherited ideas but of inherited possibilities of ideas" (1954a, ¶136). Jung (1936, ¶395) utilizes the metaphor of a dry riverbed to explain the function of archetypes, i.e., the riverbed remains even when the river is completely dry, waiting to give shape and flow when the water returns to fill the riverbed. Archetypes can also be thought of as the wire armature (i.e., underlying metal framework) over which a sculpture is molded with clay. The wire provides the interior support guiding the fundamental shape the sculpture will have, for example a horse, but there are infinite possibilities for the final appearance of the horse sculpture as the sculptor applies the clay over the wire armature.

Statistical and linguistic analysis of story lines from fiction, religions, and mythology indicates that there are between six and eight basic underlying structures to most written narratives across the world, which supports Jung's idea that there are underlying universals shaping human experience (Reagan et al. 2016). The main figures, situation, and contextual details differ in these stories, but the underlying structure of these narratives remains relatively consistent. Jung explains this underlying commonality through his concept of the archetype as innate pattern rather than through traditional explanatory models, e.g., direct transmission and migration, or by convergence, i.e., a reflection of cultural and environmental influences or pressures resulting in similar patterns of narrative emerging within disparate groups.

Jung also establishes a close relationship between archetypes and instincts, with Jung seeing archetypes as being associated more with psychological and spiritual experience while the instincts are more closely associated with somatic experience. Jung classified the instincts as follows: "From the psychological standpoint five main groups of instinctive factors can be distinguished: hunger, sexuality, activity, reflection, and creativity" (1936/1937,

¶246). Clearly, this is a departure from Freud who identified two primary instincts, Eros (sexuality), into which he subsumed the instinct for self-preservation, and Thanatos (death instinct),[1] and from Melanie Klein who expanded Freud's concept of Thanatos to include a much greater emphasis on aggression as a component of the innate destructiveness of the death drive.

Jung speaks of instinct and archetype as nearly synonymous in nature. He states, "The primordial image [archetype] might suitably be described as the instinct's perception of itself, or as the self-portrait of the instinct" (1919, ¶277). Later, Jung makes this point even more explicit, "the archetypes are the unconscious images of the instincts themselves; in other words, they are patterns of instinctive behavior" (1936, ¶91). Finally, Jung indicates that archetypes also serve as instinctual release mechanisms, "the collective contents expressed in mythologems represent such situational patterns which are so intimately connected with the release of instinct" (1945, ¶208). The three papers which provide the most in-depth discussion of the link between archetype and instinct are *Instinct and the Unconscious* (Jung 1919), *On the Nature of the Psyche* (Jung 1954b), and *Psychological Factors in Human Behavior* (Jung 1936/1937).

Jung makes a distinction between the archetype and the archetypal image. This is a significant distinction which is frequently overlooked, both within the Jungian analytic community and in the utilization of Jung's terminology in popular culture. As Jung's terminology has been adopted within popular culture, the distinction between archetype and archetypal image has eroded. The archetype proper is not visible to conscious perception, it is essentially unknown and unknowable, the presence and influence of the archetype is only inferred indirectly through collective patterns such as religious motifs, myths, fairy tales, alchemical texts, literature, and art, or through images appearing in dreams:

An archetypal content expresses itself … in metaphors. If such a content should speak of the sun and identify with it the lion, the king, the hoard of gold guarded by the dragon, or the power that makes for the life and health of man, it is neither the one thing nor the other, but the unknown third thing that finds more or less adequate expression in all these similes, yet – to the perpetual vexation of the intellect – remains unknown and not to be fitted into a formula. ... Not for a moment dare we succumb to the illusion that an archetype can be finally explained and disposed of. Even the best attempts at explanation are only more or less successful translations into another metaphorical language.

(Jung 1951, ¶267, 271)

Jung uses the phrase 'archetypal image' to describe an archetypal pattern that has taken on specific form, become perceptible, and entered the field of consciousness, "The actualized archetype appears as an archetypal image, representation, or process, and its form may change continuously according to the constellation in which it occurs" (Jacobi 1973, p. 40). In Jung's words:

The archetypal representations (images and ideas) mediated to us by the unconscious should not be confused with the archetype as such. They are very varied structures which all point back to one essentially "irrepresentable" basic form. The latter is characterized by certain formal elements and by certain fundamental meanings although these can be grasped only approximately.

(1954b, ¶417)

However, Jung himself was not always consistent in his use of his own terminology and sometimes uses archetype and archetypal image interchangeably.

When an archetypal image appears in a dream, or through some other process, Jung indicates that it carries with it an intensification of psychic energy and a feeling of numinosity. Numinosity is a term Jung adopted from Otto (1923/1965) which Otto used to describe the experience of awe associated with profound or deep spiritual experience. Jung describes the experience of emerging archetypal material as follows, "When an archetype appears in a dream, in a fantasy, or in life, it always brings with it a certain influence or power by virtue of which it either exerts a numinous or fascinating effect, or impels to action" (1917, ¶109), and "The archetype is … a *dynamism* which makes itself felt in the numinosity and fascinating power of the archetypal image" (1954b, ¶414, italics in original).

Archetype of the Self

For Jung, the most significant archetype is the Self. In Jung's model, the Self is the central ordering principle of the psyche, both its center and its totality, "The self is not only the centre but also the whole circumference which embraces both conscious and unconscious; it is the centre of this totality, just as the ego is the centre of the conscious mind" (Jung 1968, ¶44). A more encompassing definition provides a better idea of the scope of experience and function Jung associates with the Self:

> The self designates the whole range of psychic phenomena in man. It expresses the unity of the personality as a whole. But in so far as the total personality, on account of its unconscious component, can be only in part conscious, the concept of the self is, in part, only *potentially* empirical and is to that extent a *postulate*. In other words, it encompasses both the experienceable and the inexperienceable (or the not yet experienced). … In so far as psychic totality, consisting of both conscious and unconscious contents, is a postulate, it is a *transcendental* concept, for it presupposes the existence of unconscious factors on empirical grounds and thus characterizes an entity that can be described only in part but, for the other part, remains at present unknowable and illimitable.
> (Jung 1971, ¶789, italics in original)

Jung indicates that the Self is experienced as transcending personal subjectivity when encountered in some manifested form – such as in a dream, "Anything that man postulates as being a greater totality than himself can become a symbol of the self" (1948a, ¶232). This characteristic is seen as so powerful that Jung indicates the phenomenological experience of the Self is indistinguishable from an experience of the God-image, "But as one can never distinguish empirically between a symbol of the self and a God-image, the two ideas, however much we try to differentiate them, always appear blended together" (1948a, ¶231). Additionally, Jung indicates that the Self should not just be considered a structure of the psyche, but also a reflection of a dynamic process, "The self is not just a static quantity or constant form, but is also a dynamic process" (1959, ¶411).

Jung's use of term is not synonymous with the use of the term by Jacobson who uses the term 'self' to refer to "the whole person of an individual, including his body and body parts as well as his psychic organization and its parts" (Jacobson 1964, p. 6fn). In Kohut's self psychology, self refers to the core of the personality, the center of initiative, the recipient of impressions, and the repository of the individual's particular constellation of core or nuclear ambitions, ideals, talents, and skills. In many respects, Kohut's concept of self is closer to Jung's in terms of being conceptualized as a supraordinate structure that organizes and directs, but Kohut's model of self does not include the transcendent element Jung associates with the concept. However, in Kohut's model the self is conceptualized as possessing an innate nuclear program or inherent design awaiting a responsive milieu that will enable it to unfold (Kohut 1984), which is quite similar to Jung's conceptualization of the Self as guiding the ongoing process of development which he refers to as individuation.

The Primary Self

Within the classical Jungian framework, the Self is present, operating in the background during the first half of life during which (theoretically) one establishes one's identity and relative security in relationship with the outer world. In this model, the Self only becomes important in the second half of life, following a midlife passage, when there emerges a pull or calling to turn inwards, engaging in a deeper relationship with one's inner life. Fordham (1971, 1985) introduced a new variation in Jung's conceptualization of the Self, i.e., the primary self. The classical position in analytical psychology of the time was that the infant was fully contained by, or fused with, the mother's psyche, and therefore had no separate experience of Self. Classical Jungians also held that any psychopathology appearing in a child was solely a reflection of problems with the parents, e.g., the child was living out the shadow of the parents, especially the mother (Fordham 1993). Fordham was influenced by the work of Melanie Klein and Donald Winnicott, as well as his own experiences working with children as a psychiatrist and analyst. Fordham laid the conceptual framework for the existence of a primary self, existing from birth prior to the development of the ego, and that the primary self was an active factor in shaping childhood development. At the time, this was considered heretical to classical Jungians, but Fordham's conception of the infant/child primary self is quite consistent with contemporary research on infant/child development (e.g., Stern 1985; Beebe and Lachmann 2002). As Astor puts it,

> Fordham suggested that before there was an ego there was a primary self. This primary self he thought of as integrated, a psychosomatic potential waiting to unfold in interaction with the environment. The primary self expressed itself through actions which brought it into contact with the environment.
>
> (1995, p. 53)

Clinical Example of Archetypal Themes

The following brief vignettes are intended to illustrate how archetypal (i.e., universal or 'impersonal') themes are often interwoven with personal themes (see also Whitmont 1987; Williams 1963). The patient, Kathy, was a twenty-eight-year-old white female who presented with anorexia and obsessive-compulsive disorder.

Kathy began reporting her dreams approximately three months into the analysis. She said, "This is the first time I've had this dream in years." According to Kathy this was a recurring dream she has had since childhood.

> *I'm playing outside in my front yard. A mysterious person drives up. He's in an old beat-up car. I can tell he's going to kidnap me. I'm trying to get inside, but the door is locked. Just as I'm about to get in he takes me.*

While there are many possibilities present in the dream, there is an archetypal parallel with the Hades–Persephone myth in which the young maiden Persephone is innocently picking flowers in a field when she is kidnapped, taken into the Underworld, and raped by Hades.

Kathy stood in front of her garbage disposal each night, carefully examining the portion of food she had placed on her plate. Almost always her anxiety was elevated, and she felt compelled to throw part of her food down the disposal. From an archetypal perspective, as Kathy engaged in this behavior, she was unconsciously influenced by the archetypal patterns associated with Prometheus who decides what food belongs to the gods and what should be given to humankind. Like Prometheus, whose liver was devoured by a vulture each day, Kathy paid for her offenses against the gods of her inner world (persecutory internal objects) by being hollowed out both physically and psychically. Her body now reflects the emptiness that had been constellated psychologically.

At the same time, she was perhaps also unconsciously identified with an archetypal pattern reflected in the myth of Tantalus whose hunger can never be addressed. As punishment for deceiving the goddess Demeter, Tantalus was cast into the Underworld where he remains forever in the middle of a waist-deep lake. Hanging over him are trees laden with pears, pomegranates, apples, and sweet figs. However, each time Tantalus attempts to satisfy his hunger, the winds toss the limbs of trees out his reach, and each time he bends down to quench his thirst, the cool waters recede. Thus, he stands forever, in the midst of plenty, his desires never satisfied.

Archetypes – Parallels with other Psychoanalytic Ideas

Two prominent figures in psychoanalysis also proposed concepts which parallel Jung's concept of the archetype – Melanie Klein and Wilfred Bion. Klein departed from Freud along some of the same lines as Jung. Klein proposed that the primary contents of the mind are inextricably bound up with the instincts, in fact, that they are the mental representations of instincts (Urban 1992). Klein's concept of 'unconscious phantasies' is quite similar to Jung's concept of archetypes. She writes, "I believe that phantasies operate from the outset, as do the instincts, and are the mental expression of the activity of both the life and death instincts"

(Klein 1952, p. 52). Isaacs offers a more complete elaboration of the relationship between phantasies and instincts than Klein, one that is quite similar to Jung's description of the relationship between archetypes and instincts. Isaacs states that, "phantasies are the primary content of unconscious mental processes. ... This 'mental expression' of instinct is unconscious phantasy. Phantasy is (in the first instance) the mental corollary, the psychic representative, of instinct" (1948, pp. 82–83).

Isaacs (1948, p. 94) indicates that the infant has a knowledge of the breast that is "inherent," and which is "the aim of instinct." Hence, both Jung and Isaacs emphasize that there is an image that exists within the psyche which facilitates the instinct in recognizing what it seeks. Solomon underscores the parallels between Jung's concept of archetype and Klein's concept of unconscious fantasy, referring to both concepts as "deep structural categories which mediate the experiences of the real baby and his mother" (Solomon 1991, p. 309).

The idea that there is a pre-structuring of unconscious experience also appears in Bion's work in terms of his concept of 'pre-conception' (Bion 1993). In Bion's model, infants are born with pre-conceptions. The infant searches for and eventually finds realizations of these pre-conceptions in the outer world, a search essential to survival. An example of this would be the infant's innate search for the mother's breast. When a pre-conception encounters a realization in the world of the pre-conception, a 'conception' is created in the infant's field of experience. As Bion frames the issue,

> Why should there not be what we would call mental vestiges, or archaic elements, which are operative in a way that is alarming and disturbing because it breaks through the beautiful calm surface we ordinarily think of as rational, sane behavior?
>
> (Bion 1994, p. 236)

When asked whether there was a similarity between Bion's notion of pre-conceptions and Jung's notion of archetypes, Grotstein responded, "I think quite a bit. In fact, I think it's the same thing.

Preconceptions, like archetypes, intuit, anticipate their future"
(Grotstein in Culbert-Koehn 1997, p. 29).

Collective Unconscious

Jung's concept of a collective unconscious refers to an impersonal
or universal unconscious carried or shared as potentials by all
human beings, i.e., an influence from the unconscious which is not
derived from personal experience and the environment. Jung
sometimes used the term 'objective psyche' synonymously with
collective unconscious, choosing this term to describe contents of
the psyche that originate from an objective source, i.e., outside or
beyond the limits of individual experience, rather than of a personal or subjective nature. Jung saw mythology, religion, fairy tales,
and alchemy as a reflection of the collective unconscious, "The
whole of mythology could be taken as a sort of projection of the
collective unconscious" (1931b, ¶325).

In terms of the reassimilation or acceptance of Jung and analytical psychology by psychoanalysts from other schools of
thought, I would suggest the concept of the collective unconscious
is the single greatest obstacle to the acceptance of Jung and analytical psychology. However, Jung's concept of a collective unconscious is not quite as removed from Freud's theories as it is often
portrayed. Freud's *Totem and Taboo* (1913) and *Moses and
Monotheism* (1939) are structured around Freud's ideas regarding
phylogenetic inheritance (Hoffer 1992). Additionally, a missing
and unpublished paper by Freud written in 1912, "Overview of the
Transference Neuroses," was discovered by Ilse Grubrich-Simitis
in 1983 in a trunk belonging to the estate of Sandor Ferenczi
(Grubrich-Simitis 1987; Garcia 1988). In the paper, Freud proposes that the neuroses observed in his patients may have originated as adaptive responses of the entire species to threatening
environmental changes or to traumatic events in the prehistory of
humankind – which are activated in the present through phylogenetic mnemic traces. In the "Overview" paper, Freud asserts that
"the inherited dispositions are residues of the acquisitions of our
ancestors" and that neuroses somehow "bear witness to the history of the mental development of mankind" (quoted in Garcia

1988, p. 91). Bearing Freud's theory of phylogenetic traces in mind, Jung's concept of the collective unconscious may seem less implausible to those from other psychoanalytic traditions.

Quite similar to Freud, Jung indicates that the collective unconscious is "the ancestral heritage of possibilities of representation" (1931b, ¶321) and "consists of the sum of the instincts and their correlates, the archetypes. Just as everybody possesses instincts, so he also possesses a stock of archetypal images" (1919, ¶281). Elsewhere, Jung asserts that "the archetypes are the unconscious images of the instincts themselves; in other words, they are patterns of instinctive behavior. The hypothesis of the collective unconscious is, therefore, no more daring than to assume that there are instincts" (1936, ¶91–92). Jung also emphasizes that the contents of the collective unconscious are not a result of the repression barrier,

> the contents of the collective unconscious have never been in consciousness, and therefore have never been individually acquired, but owe their existence exclusively to heredity. Whereas the personal unconscious consists for the most part of complexes, the content of the collective unconscious is made up essentially of archetypes.
>
> (1936, ¶88)

Critiques of Archetype and Collective Unconscious

From within the field of analytical psychology, there has emerged during the past two decades a number of critiques, challenges, and revisioning of Jung's concepts of archetype and the collective unconscious. These critiques address both concepts jointly because they are grounded in an assumption of innate, a priori elements of experience. Most of the critiques revisit these concepts from the perspective of emergence theory, developmental research, dynamic systems models, and new developments in neurosciences.

In particular, these critiques challenge the validity of the innate, pre-existing origin of archetypal experience and therefore also of the existence of a collective unconscious. For example, Merchant (2006, 2009) proposes that the experiences currently attributed to innate factors in the psyche can also be explained through an emergent/developmental model,

> which sees archetypal imagery as an emergent phenomenon arising out of neural bio-structures laid down in early infant life as a result of developmental experience. This model is supported by the current findings of those developmental biologists who adhere to Developmental Systems Theory ... the model ... leads to a new perspective on innatism; it implies an archetype–environment nexus; it collapses the nature–nurture debate in relation to archetype theory; it collapses the 'sacred heritage' approach to archetypes, and it removes the conceptual division between the collective and personal unconscious.
>
> (2006, p. 125)

Hogenson (2009, 2019) draws more heavily on neuroscience, particularly the discovery of mirror neurons as part of the non-cognitive processing network that facilitates the experience of empathy. He places Jung's concepts within the intellectual climate in which Jung's ideas developed and proposes that we may not require the concept of a dynamic unconscious at all:

> Jung, of course, was still an heir to the western intellectual tradition wedded to the notion that some pre-existing plan had to underlie the emergence of phenomenal experience, the proximate form of this tradition – at least for the early psychoanalysts – being the dynamic unconscious. And so, we have the Jungian theory of the collective unconscious. I now want to suggest that just as theoretical robotics, complex dynamic systems theories of development, and the discovery of mirror neurons have concluded that it is possible to develop complex behavioural patterns without the cognitive processor embedded somewhere in the brain/mind, that we may be in a position to do without the dynamic unconscious as an explanatory hypothesis. Rather, we may be looking at the historical emergence of human behaviour from the interactive engagement with the ... species typical environment. The unconscious, then,

would be more a matter of what we have yet to encounter, rather than that which lies below, either in the form of repressions or collective forms.

(Hogenson 2009, p. 334)

Knox (2001, 2003, 2004) also proposes an emergent/developmental model based on the explanatory vehicle of 'image schemas,' introduced by developmental researchers, which can be understood as foundational mind/brain structures which are acquired developmentally during the period of pre-verbal experience. Image schemas are conceptually quite similar to Stern's (1985) concept of 'Representations of Interactions that have been Generalized.' Knox argues that archetypes are "emergent structures resulting from a developmental interaction between genes and environment that is unique for each person. Archetypes are not 'hard-wired' collections of universal imagery waiting to be released by the right environmental trigger" (2004, p. 4). Following from this premise Knox offers the following conclusion,

Whilst image schemas are without symbolic content in themselves, they provide a reliable scaffolding on which meaningful imagery and thought is organized and constructed. … If we adopt this model for archetypes, we have to discard the view that they are genetically inherited and consider them to be reliably repeated early developmental achievements.

(2004, p. 9)

Brooke (2015, p. 144), working from an existential phenomenological perspective, arrives at a similar, succinctly stated position, "Archetypes structure experience, they do not produce it" (2015, p. 144). In other words, Brooke indicates that archetypes (and the collective unconscious) should not be interpreted as a generator of images, but rather as an organizer of experience.

Taking up the question of inherited archetypal structures, Goodwyn (2021) argues that it is a false dichotomy to frame the origin of archetypes as innate, biologically emergent, or culturally transmitted. In his conclusion, summarizing the state of contemporary neuroscience in relationship with analytical psychology, Goodwyn states:

The evidence we have now shows that the human mind does indeed have a strong predisposition to make the associations found in catalogues of recurrent symbolism, just as Jung proposed, but this has little to do with cultural transmission. Rather, this is due to a combination of biological predispositions acted upon by intense internally directed but universally achieved learning, which is itself biologically based and continuously supported. As I see it, I don't think Jung could have hoped for any better confirmation of his theory.

(2021, pp. 126–127)

Colman (2021) provides one of the most comprehensive and compelling critiques and reappraisals of Jung's concepts of archetype, the collective unconscious, and symbol. In *Act and Image* Colman draws from philosophy, phenomenology, developmental psychology, neuroscience, linguistics, archaeology, and anthropology and critically reflects on commonly held assumptions regarding these concepts. Colman deconstructs these assumptions and offers a new interpretation which sees the psyche as developing from humans' engagement with their relational and material environment. Thus, Colman argues that archetypal experience is not delivered to us from an unseen reservoir of image potentials but is an emergent phenomenon that results from active engagement with a world that is already imbued with meaning. Through his line of reasoning, Colman aims to move past the traditional dichotomy set up between cultural versus biological transmission in terms of the origins of universal experiences. While he rejects Jung's hypothesis of a collective unconscious made up of archetypal forms, Colman does not see this as a wholesale rejection of Jung's opus, but as an extension of Jung's life-long fascination with the symbolic imagination of the human species.

Roesler provides a stark summary of the current state of Jung's archetypal theory in light of contemporary critique, "There is a strong consensus of experts dealing with archetype theory in the last two decades … that Jung's assumption of a biological/genetic transmission of archetypes can no longer be supported" (2019, p. 662). Roesler (2019) also indicates that some of the critics of archetypal patterns, particularly those making use of dynamic systems theory, argue that instead of conceptualizing archetypes as structures, they would be better regarded as universal processes.

Elsewhere, Roesler offers a broader assessment of the current situation in analytical psychology:

> Central parts of the classical concept, like the idea of genetic transmission from generation to generation, the idea of universality, and also the extent of what can be taken as archetypal, are fundamentally in question … neither practitioners nor educational structures have taken this enough into account. In Jungian publications, Jung's classical argumentation can still be found unquestioned. … If at present, the classical Jungian ideas of how alleged archetypal patterns are passed from generation to generation in such a way that their universality is assured for all people in all cultures, is by no means backed by contemporary scientific insight, then archetype theory as a central building block of analytical psychology is questionable. On the other hand, the concept can be productively worked with in clinical environments as well as in the analysis of cultural phenomena.
>
> (2022, pp. 190–191)

Roesler's last point is significant because he makes a distinction between the theoretical understanding of the concepts of archetype and the collective unconscious and the clinical utilization of these concepts.

As a clinician, I have arrived at a similar perspective, i.e., in my analytic practice I am not concerned with the origins or source of imagery as it emerges. I am interested in the effect it has on my patient and the analytic process. In my analytic practice, supervision, teaching, and my writing (Winborn 2019, 2020), I have adopted the position that engagement with archetypal material is significant and transformative because all archetypal imagery potentially functions as metaphor, just as images arising in dreams and fantasies is often expressed through metaphor. For example, with the case example of Kathy presented earlier, the origin of the archetypal motifs found in her dreams and behaviors is not essential, but the utility of these images as metaphors for understanding Kathy and in the formulation of interpretive interventions is important. As contemporary cognitive science and neuroscience have demonstrated, metaphor impacts individuals in a profoundly affective and transformative manner, much different than the reaction to ordinary prose.

Ultimately, the question regarding the nature and origin of archetypal patterns is more essential from a theoretical perspective than in the context of how the analyst practices clinically. For the purposes of an analytic process, it is the archetype as experience (i.e., the phenomenology of archetypal experience, descriptive of an element emerging in the analytic field, intra-psychically, or in life) that is most essential rather than the origins of archetypal images or themes. In other words, archetypal patterns which possess a quality of 'something more' than ordinary experience can be effectively utilized to describe or engage with experiences of the patient and the analytic dyad. A theoretical position regarding the origin of archetypes is not necessary for the use of the concept as a descriptive category of experience. Experiences having a ring of universality, inherent order, or transcendence to them can be engaged without necessitating an attribution about the 'location' or origin of these experiences. In the clinical setting, the focus is on the immediacy and quality of the experience, just as Otto (1923/1965) articulated numinosity and awe as qualities of religious experience. Similarly, the introduction of archetypal motifs into the analytic setting can be functionally effective and transformative regardless of the theoretical genesis of archetypal experience.

Finally, Mills (2018) evaluates Jung's concept of the collective unconscious from a philosophical perspective and argues that Jung's argument for the existence of a universal, collective influence which transcends the personal psyche cannot be supported from a philosophical perspective. In his conclusion, Mills states:

> Jung's prediction that the collective psyche is an explication for the phenomena in question is to presuppose the existence of the very thing that needs an explanation; hence he is begging the question. When he reverts to archetypes as the products of a collective unconscious, he makes them synonymous with the collective and hence their ontic manifestation is causally conditioned on the original presupposition of a collective Mind. And when Jung theoretically justifies collective

phenomena oozing from an originating collective ground, this collapses into tautology. Here we may say that the collective unconscious is tantamount to a myth as explanans for it provides a story – of origins, of functions, of structures inherent to human mental processes. In fact, the generalization and reification, if not deification, of the collective unconscious has generated its own myth among many Jungians where a collective psyche is thought to maintain its own ontological independence, which thereby grounds, conditions, and is the foundation of all productions of consciousness, supervenes on our subjective minds through supernatural means such as emanationism, and is of divine provenance, namely, the presence or derivative of the mind of God.

(2018, p. 13)

Certainly, Mills provides a well-reasoned argument in his critique, yet it is an argument made from the logical, rational position of analytic philosophy as opposed to the approach someone from the tradition of continental philosophy, particularly a phenomenological philosopher might make. According to Groden and Kreiswirth:

Phenomenology is a philosophy of experience. For phenomenology the ultimate source of all meaning and value is the lived experience of human beings. All philosophical systems, scientific theories, or aesthetic judgments have the status of abstractions from the ebb and flow of the lived world. The task of the philosopher, according to phenomenology, is to describe the structures of experience, in particular consciousness, the imagination, relations with other persons, and the situatedness of the human subject in society and history.

(1994, p. 562)

As Brooke (2000, 2015) points out, Jung's work is fundamentally grounded in experience and is therefore much more compatible with a philosophy of experience such as phenomenology, particularly existential phenomenology. Brooke succinctly summarizes Jung's approach to psychological experience in this way, "Jung's hermeneutic approach, with its phenomenological emphases on receptivity to phenomena as immediately presented and continually self-revealing, is appropriate to his views of psychological life and therapeutic work" (Brooke 2015, p. 180).

Note

1 Freud's concept of Thanatos was influenced by but not credited to earlier work by Sabina Spielrein (1912/1994). See Van Waning (1992) and Caropreso (2017).

Suggestions for Further Reading

Classic Papers

Archetypes

Jung, C.G. (1934/1954). Archetypes of the collective unconscious. In *CW9i*. Princeton, NJ: Princeton University Press.

Collective Unconscious

Jung, C.G. (1936). On the concept of the collective unconscious. In *CW9i*. Princeton, NY: Princeton University Press.

Additional Readings

Archetypes and the Collective Unconscious

Colman, W. (2021). *Act and Image: The Emergence of Symbolic Imagination*. London: Routledge.
Roesler, C. (2022). *C.G. Jung's Archetype Concept: Theory, Research and Applications*. London: Routledge.
Stevens, A. (2015). *Archetype Revisited: An Updated Natural History of the Self*. London: Routledge.

Alchemy

Edinger, E. (1985). *Anatomy of the Psyche: Alchemical Symbolism in Psychotherapy*. La Salle, IL: Open Court.

Mythology

Edinger, E. (1994). *The Eternal Drama: The Inner Meaning of Greek Mythology.* Boston, MA: Shambhala.

Fairy Tales

von Franz, M.L. (1970). *Interpretation of Fairy Tales.* Dallas, TX: Spring Publications.

Chapter 4

Jungian Complex Theory

What is a Complex?

Jung's concept of complexes is the most essential element in the theory and practice of analytical psychology. Complex theory is so central to Jung's model that he initially considered naming his new approach to psychoanalysis 'complex psychology' rather than analytical psychology. Whereas archetypes and instincts make up the collective aspect of unconscious experience, complexes largely reflect the contents of personal unconscious. Some commonly encountered complexes include the mother, father, authority, inferiority, victim, hero, child, savior, and money complexes.

Complexes are seen as the fundamental structures which organize the human psyche around specific themes, relationships, and situations. They can also be thought of as discrete centers of energy within the psyche. Complex links both personal and archetypal components of individual experience, bridging the intrapsychic and the interpersonal, affecting both inner and outer relationships (subjective and objective), in an interwoven manner. Complexes are formed, partially, through interactions with other individuals, the surrounding culture, and through various experiences in life. As these complexes develop as part the individual's internal structure, they begin to influence the individual's perceptions of and interactions with the outer world, as well as their inner world.

The psyche can be conceived of as a network of complexes possessing both adaptive, progressive aspects of the psyche as well

DOI: 10.4324/9781003223511-5

as maladaptive, regressive aspects. In short, the network of complexes consists "of inner working models, affects and expectation patterns that are primarily saved in the implicit memory and are partially conscious but mostly unconscious" (Bovensiepen, 2006, p. 458). An adequately developed ego complex and the self-structure form the core sub-network responsible for the cohesion and regulation of the psychological system (Dieckmann, 1999).

Jung began to develop his theory of complexes during his early career as a psychiatrist at the Burghölzli Psychiatric Hospital while doing research with the word association test (WAT) between 1903 and 1907. Briefly, the WAT is a series of one hundred stimulus words which are read aloud to the subject. The subject is asked to respond to the stimulus word with the first word that comes into their thoughts (i.e., their association). The experimenter records the responses and records the length of time it took for the subject to respond. In Jung's research protocol the subject's somatic response was also recorded using a skin galvanometer. After the subject's responses are recorded, the subject is then asked to recall their responses to the initial stimulus words. Jung observed that different stimulus words produced different responses for different subjects, as well as different patterns in terms of ability to reproduce their original response. His reflections on these response patterns led to his conceptualization of complexes as a central organizing structure the psyche. Over time these characteristic difficulties were standardized into eighteen 'complex indicators' – such as prolonged reaction time in comparison to the mean response time, incorrect reproduction of the subject's initial response, mishearing, slips of the tongue, and so on. Jung came to recognize that certain stimulus words were triggers for unconscious affective activation which was manifested through the complex indicators. A protocol was developed for evaluating and categorizing the stimulus words that resulted in the most complex indicators for each subject. Post-experiment debriefing with subjects often revealed the narrative underlying these clusters of complex indicators.

As mentioned in Chapter 1, Jung was excited because he felt his research with the WAT (Jung 1973a) provided support for Freud's theory of repression. As his series of experiments progressed, Jung came to realize that the WAT also established an empirical basis for his emerging theory of complexes. After his split from Freud, Jung utilized his theory of complexes to differentiate his analytic model from Freud's, e.g., "The via regia to the unconscious, however, is not the dream, as he [Freud] thought, but the complex, which is the architect of dreams and of symptoms" (1958, ¶210). Elsewhere he states, "Freud is seeking the complexes, I am not … I am looking for what the unconscious is doing with the complexes" (1935, ¶175). While Freud did adopt Jung's term 'complexes,' Jung first introduced the term 'complex' in 1904, "By 'emotionally charged complex' we mean the sum of ideas referring to a particular feeling toned event" (1973a, ¶167 fn18). Throughout his writing Jung refers to complexes in several different ways: as splinter psyches, miniature self-contained psyches, fragmentary personalities, dissociated personalities, and unconscious fantasy systems. He highlights the autonomous nature of the complexes which are frequently experienced as personified elements of the psyche, "Every autonomous or even relatively autonomous complex has the peculiarity of appearing as a personality, i.e., of being personified" (1966, ¶312). By 'autonomous,' Jung means that the activated complex operates independently from the conscious will of the ego. Jung also points out that the complex will be experienced subjectively as something alien or other, "it also involves an experience of a special kind namely the recognition of an alien 'other' in oneself, or the objective presence of another will" (1967, ¶481). In a more comprehensive statement, Jung indicates a complex is:

> the image of a certain psychic situation which is strongly accentuated emotionally and is, moreover, incompatible with the habitual attitude of consciousness. This image has a powerful inner coherence, it has its own wholeness and, in addition, a relatively high degree of autonomy, so that it is subject to the control of the conscious mind only to a limited extent, and therefore behaves like an animated foreign body in the sphere of consciousness.
>
> (1948b, ¶201)

For Jung, his concept of complexes is central to his understanding of symptoms and psychopathology. Jung makes a direct link between dissociative defenses, the development of complexes, and their manifestation through neurotic symptoms, "A neurosis is a dissociation of personality due to the existence of complexes" (1935, ¶382). However, he also saw the complex as pointing the way towards a 'cure,' with the development of neurotic symptoms as an attempt at self-cure by a self-regulating psyche, "It is an attempt of the self-regulating psychic system to restore balance, in no way different from the function of dreams" (1935, ¶389).

The idea of the complex is a robust clinical concept for the practicing therapist/psychoanalyst. An understanding of one's complexes is also a means of orienting within one's individual path towards wholeness, the process which Jung refers to as individuation. Complexes are naturally occurring psychological phenomena which typically develop along positive or negative lines. In therapy, it is usually the negative aspects of a complex which are encountered. However, a complex configured along the positive pole of experience can be just as life sustaining as a negatively configured complex can be destructive. And yet, when taken to an extreme, even a positive complex can be limiting or destructive.

Complexes are often represented in dreams as figures, which Jung refers to as personification, i.e., referring to a recurrent psychological process which becomes depicted in dreams as a figure or series of similar figures, e.g.:

> The peculiar thing about these dissociations is that the split-off personality is not just a random one, but stands in a complementary or compensatory relationship to the ego-personality. It is a personification of traits of character which are sometimes worse and sometimes better than those the ego-personality possesses.
>
> (Jung 1969, ¶468)

But a complex can also be represented by the context, actions, objects, and situations portrayed in a dream.

Jung conceptualizes complexes as having an archetypal core (e.g., the Great Mother) with a personalistic overlay or shell (e.g., the internalized or introjected experience of the personal mother). Jung also posits that archetypes tend to constellate around poles of experience, either positively or negatively, i.e., the bipolarity of the archetype (Jung 1959/1969, ¶413). As a result of the bipolar archetypal core at the center of the complex, complexes will tend to be valanced either positively or negatively. The personalistic 'shell' of the complex is a patterned amalgam of experience impressions and response patterns made up of images, memories, feelings and affects, physiological states, thought patterns or cognitive sets, attitudes, defense mechanisms,[1] behavioral patterns, activating events, patterns of object relatedness, and attachment style. Bovensiepen understands "the complex shells as a fall-out of later developmental, emotional and interpersonal experiences with significant others" (2006, p. 452). Differentiating the elements of a complex is useful to the analyst in terms of identifying particular aspects of the complex to engage interpretatively, in an effort to create links between various conscious and unconscious aspects of experience (see Figure 4.1).

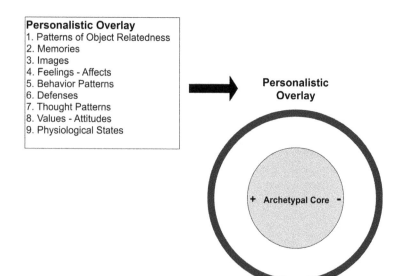

Figure 4.1 Diagram of a complex.

Functional Complexes

There are some complexes that are seen frequently in the clinical setting – particularly mother, father, and child complexes. But despite the relatively high frequency of appearance, the complex will be manifest differently in each person. Additionally, there are often other complexes, seen less frequently which are unique to each individual, i.e., a complex may emerge or be created/constellated around any significant relationship or situation. However, Jung also proposed that everyone has four complexes which function similarly in everyone's psyche. These four complexes – ego, shadow, persona, and anima/animus – are referred to as functional complexes.

Ego Complex

Jung's use of the term ego is essentially the same as Freud's, but in Jung's conceptualization of complexes each complex has a corresponding archetype at its core. In terms of the ego, Jung proposed that the archetypal center of the ego complex is the Self. Jung defines the ego as follows: "By ego I understand a complex of ideas which constitutes the centre of my field of consciousness and appears to possess a high degree of continuity and identity" (1971, ¶706) and "The ego is a complex … that peculiar complex whose inner cohesion amounts to consciousness" (1960/1969, ¶614). However, despite its prominent position in the psyche, when other complexes are activated, these autonomous auxiliary complexes have the capacity to temporarily push the ego complex out of the primary role it plays as the center of consciousness (Jung, 1960/1969, ¶201).

Jung often associated the mythological motif of the hero's journey with the developmental arc of the ego. In this motif the hero's task is characterized as: leave his established community (i.e., differentiate), do battle with an opposing force, monster, or ruler of a foreign land (e.g., engage and defeat the father complex), or slay the dragon (defeat the mother complex), and be transformed by the experience before returning to his community to take up a new and more mature role or position. Some have challenged the suitability of this motif for women's developmental hurdles and have offered alternative interpretations, often characterized as the heroine's journey (e.g., Murdock 1990; Woodman 1992).

Shadow Complex

The shadow complex is conceptualized as the repository for all things rejected by the ego and undeveloped in the psyche (Jacobi 1973, p. 111). Therefore, the shadow complex stands in direct relationship to the ego complex. Psychological material which conflicts with the sense of identity associated with the ego complex is repressed or otherwise defended against emerging. However, undeveloped aspects of the psyche which have not had a supportive environment which facilitates their development can also become associated with shadow, even when these elements of self-experience have never come into consciousness. From Jung's perspective, the goal in terms of the shadow complex is to bring into consciousness, accept, and integrate the elements associated with the shadow complex:

> The shadow is a moral problem that challenges the whole ego-personality, for no one can become conscious of the shadow without considerable moral effort. To become conscious of it involves recognizing the dark aspects of the personality as present and real.
>
> (1959, ¶14)

Jung also differentiates between a personal or individual shadow complex and a collective shadow. The collective shadow refers to the hidden antithesis of the prevailing Zeitgeist (Jacobi 1973, p. 111). Additionally, in a somewhat confusing manner, Jung refers to shadow in two different ways in his writing. The most common usage is the narrow definition of shadow as the unwanted aspects of the personality which are disavowed by the ego complex. Less frequently, Jung uses the term shadow very broadly, to refer to almost any aspect of experience that is unconscious.

Persona Complex

The persona complex functions as the mediator between the ego and the outer world (the object) and is often the outward manifestation of the ego ideal, and the outward manifestation of the persona adopted may vary from one situation to another. It is the psychological mask worn in interaction with others that conveys how we wish to be seen with others, or it conveys our interpretation/sense of what the society or culture perceives as desirable characteristics. In Jung's words:

> The persona is a functional complex which has come into existence for reasons of adaptation or necessary convenience, but by no means is it identical with the individuality. The functional complex of the persona is exclusively concerned with relation to the object.
>
> (1971, ¶801)

While Jung sees the development of an adequate persona(s) as a necessity for adapting in life, he warns about the possibility of becoming identified with one's persona, i.e., coming to believe that we are the mask we have constructed (both consciously and unconsciously) for public consumption:

> The construction of a collectively suitable persona means a formidable concession to the external world, a genuine self-sacrifice which drives the ego straight into identification with the persona, so that people really do exist who believe they are what they pretend to be. The 'soullessness' of such an attitude is, however, only apparent, for under no circumstances will the unconscious tolerate this shifting of the centre of gravity.
>
> (1966, ¶306)

We can also speak of having a rigidly held or 'thick' persona complex (i.e., one that doesn't permit the other person a sufficient sense of the person behind the persona) or a 'thin' persona (i.e., one that doesn't provide a sufficient buffer in conflictual, adversarial, or stressful situations and interactions). A rigidly developed persona complex is similar to Winnicott's (1965) concept of the False Self which develops as a defense to protect the True Self from being wounded. Typically, with someone who has developed a False Self, this takes place through being overly compliant, appeasing, deferential, or placating to avoid the other person's potential anger, hostility, or rejection.

Anima/Animus Complex

The anima/animus complex functions as the mediator between the ego and the unconscious and is sometimes referred to by Jung as the personification of the unconscious or the soul. In fact, both anima and animus are associated with soul in Latin, but animus is more closely associated with mind and spirit. However, Jung utilizes the term anima to refer to the unconscious, compensatory contrasexual, i.e., feminine, aspect of a man's psyche and utilizes animus complex to describe the unconscious, compensatory contrasexual, i.e., masculine, aspect of a woman's psyche (1959, ¶27). Jung also associates different characteristics to the anima of a man and the animus of a woman:

> If, therefore, we speak of the anima of a man, we must logically speak of the animus of a woman, if we are to give the soul of a woman its right name. Whereas logic and objectivity are usually the predominant features of a man's outer attitude, or are at least regarded as ideals, in the case of a woman it is feeling. But in the soul, it is the other way round: inwardly it is the man who feels, and the woman who reflects.
>
> (1971, ¶805)

Jung indicates that both the shadow and the anima/animus complexes are most often projected onto others. With the shadow this typically results in negative reactions towards the person carrying the projection, and when the anima/animus is being projected it often results in attraction and desire. However, in Jung's conceptualization, if these projections are not withdrawn the elements of the psyche being projected are not available for our own development, transformation, integration, and movement towards wholeness (see Jung 1959, pp. 11–22, for a fuller perspective on the anima/animus complex).

Even with this brief introduction to Jung's anima/animus complex, it is readily seen that many of his ideas are rooted in or conflated with the culturally determined masculine and female gender roles of his time. While Jung indicates that he is not speaking about gender characteristics, there are numerous critics of his anima/animus conceptualization because gender characteristics filter into his thought process and the theory becomes quite convoluted. Critical concerns have been raised in terms of the implications of the anima/animus concept for gender identity, feminist issues, and sexual orientation (e.g., Downing 1991; Hopcke 1991; Kulkarni 1997; McKenzie 2006; von Raffay 2000; and Wehr 1987). For example, how does the notion of an inner contrasexual figure, i.e., the anima complex, apply in the situation of a gay male? As the world becomes less defined by binary categories of gender and sexual orientation, these criticisms have increased.

Apart from the concerns about Jung's conceptualization of the anima/animus concept, it is also such a difficult concept to utilize clinically. In a seminar I attended with Peter Mudd, a Jungian analyst whose area of expertise is the chronological study of Jung's *Collected Works*, he indicated that in Jung's original conceptualization of the anima/animus, these terms were only used as designations for 'soul,' reflecting the Latin meaning of these terms. Mudd indicated that when Jung began to associate the notion of the contrasexual element with these concepts, the entire concept became hopelessly muddled as a clinically viable concept in analysis. Samuels arrives at a similar conclusion to Mudd:

I do not see animus and anima as a sort of little man or little woman in the mind of a woman or man, respectively. I tend to mute the contrasexual aspect. Instead, what I highlight is the way in which a being (actually, an image) with an other anatomy carries psychological potential for the subject. So, I do not dream of a woman because what she does in my dream is feminine; I dream of a woman because her otherness symbolizes what I am not yet and might become in the future.

When I dream of a man, he too might be performing this anima-like function for me (an observation that indicates the potential of post-Jungian psychology to move beyond a heterosexist or homophobic approach to depth psychology).

(Samuels 2000, pp. 407–408)

Schwartz-Salant in the first line of his paper "Anima and Animus in Jung's Alchemical Mirror" (1992) stated, "I do not find the concepts, anima and animus to be clinically useful" (p. 1). Like Mudd and Schwartz-Salant, I have not found the anima/animus concept to be useful in the clinical practice of analysis. My efforts to find ways to incorporate the concept (during the early phases of my analytic training and career) inevitably resulted in the analytic discourse becoming overly didactic, educational, abstract, and reified, without any evidence these interactions contributed to the progress of the analysis.

Relationship between Functional Complexes

For Jung, these four functional complexes also stand in relationship with each other (i.e., a functional network of complexes) with persona as the mediator between the ego and the outer world, often as a reflection of the ego ideal, while the anima/animus is conceptualized as serving as mediator between the ego and the unconscious. Persona and shadow are seen as being in compensatory relationship with each other, i.e., the brighter or more ideal the persona is, then the more difficult it will be for the contents of the shadow to become acknowledged and integrated with the ego.

James Hall (1983, pp. 71–75) offers a useful classification schema regarding the functional complexes which facilitates a shift to thinking about what they 'do,' rather than what they 'are.' Hall classifies ego and shadow complexes as identity structures because they deal with the sense of what is 'I' and what is subjectively experienced as 'not I.' He classifies the anima/animus and persona complexes as relational structures, meaning they mediate relationships internally (i.e., the anima/animus complex mediates interactions between the conscious ego and the unconscious) and externally (i.e., the persona complex mediates the relationship between the ego and the outer world).

Network of Complexes

It is not uncommon for complexes to be discussed as though they operate in isolation. In actuality, the complexes operate in interactive networks, mutually influencing each other and the ego complex. A focus on the dynamic interplay within a network of complexes better reflects Jung's dissociative model of the psyche. In other words, the analytic process is best served by considering the intrapsychic situation of the patient in terms of a matrix, network, or landscape of complexes rather than viewing complexes as individual centers of psychic activity operating in isolation.

As Bovensiepen puts it, "I suggested that we should concentrate more on the relationship entanglement among the various complexes in the unconscious and not so much on how the pathogenic complexes influence the ego" (2006, p. 451). For example, a child complex is typically co-activated with the mother and father complexes. Likewise, the mother and father complexes are linked within the psyche even if one side of the parental syzygy is activated more intensely at a particular moment. The identity structures of shadow, ego, and persona engage in an ongoing ballet of self-disavowal, identity maintenance, and cultivation of outer impressions. The soul figures of anima and animus shuttle to and fro in their mediating role between ego and the unconscious. The interaction of Self, environment, culture, and the individual's network of complexes results in the narrative structure or personal myth being lived out, as well as in shaping the individual's path of individuation (Shalit 2002).

In addition, the intrapsychic network of complexes and self-structure is also in ongoing interaction with the figures and environment of the outer world. As Fosshage puts it:

> The predominant ways in which we have come to see ourselves and ourselves in relation to others are the affect-laden thematic organisations that variably shape our experience. These affect-laden organising principles or schemas (I use the terms as equivalent) do not distort a supposed 'objective reality' but are always contributing to the construction of a subjectively experienced 'reality.'
>
> (1994, p. 267)

In reflecting upon the network of interacting complexes, it is useful, both to the clinician and the patient, to imagine the network of complexes as a play taking place on a theatrical stage with an evolving cast of actors, sets, and scenes being played out. McDougall (1985, 1989) and Karbelnig (2020) have emphasized the value of the metaphor of the dramatic stage in terms of visualizing intrapsychic and intersubjective dynamics. Jung also utilizes the metaphor of the dramatic stage in discussing dreams, "The whole dream-work is essentially subjective, and the dream is a theater in which the dreamer is himself the scene, the player, the prompter, the producer, the author, the public, and the critic" (1960/1969, ¶509). However, because it is largely unconscious, the stage populated by the network of complexes is not in full view of waking consciousness. The difficult task is learning to discern, through dream, fantasy, and inference, what is going on behind the curtain of the unconscious, which requires curiosity, intuition, and courage from both analytic participants.

Circumambulation of the Complex

Circumambulation is the term Jung coined to describe the process of going around and around one's complexes during analysis (and in life). Over time, one's perspective on the complex changes resulting in a gradual increase in one's capacity to reflect upon and gain perspective on one's complexes and the network they exist in. Becoming conscious of, interacting with, and understanding the complexes (i.e., the development of the reflection function) sets the stage for progressive depotentiation of the complexes, ideally with an accompanying assimilation of some of the complex contents into the overall structures of the ego and the Self. More specifically, the aim of this process is to increase the patient's 1) ability to recognize cues which signal the activation of a complex; 2) recognition of how the complex relates to interpersonal problems. This allows the patient to distinguish what he/she brings (via their complexes) to relationship problems versus what other people and events bring to them; 3) recognition of the power of the autonomous complexes; 4) insight into origins of the complex; 5) understanding of secondary gain aspects of symptoms as well as the symptom as effort of self-cure; 6) diminishment of the power of the complex; and 7) an acquisition of a greater range of emotional and behavioral patterns. As Dieckmann (1991, p. 166) indicates, every complex has a narrative associated with it that needs to be understood, both by the therapist/analyst and the patient. This involves understanding the past of the complex, i.e., how the complex developed; the present of the complex, i.e., how the complex impacts the patient's current experiences; and the future of the complex, i.e., where the complex is moving the patient. Jung's process of circumambulating the complex is similar in spirit to Freud's method outlined in "Remembering, Repeating and Working Through" (1914).

Developments in Complex Theory: Cultural Complex

Bovensiepen's (2006) reconceptualization of complex theory in terms of the network of complexes mentioned earlier is one of the important developments in complex theory. Another important development has been the introduction of the concept of the cultural complex. Kimbles (2000) first introduced the term 'cultural complex' to analytical psychology in 2000 but acknowledges the term has been utilized in other fields previously. Singer and Kimbles subsequently expanded the recognition and utilization of the term with their book *The Cultural Complex* (2004). The concept has quickly been adopted within the field of analytical psychology and has facilitated closer examination of the interaction between the individual, group, society, and culture. The concept of the cultural complex has been utilized to reflect on such diverse issues as race, gender, sexual orientation, poverty and income disparity, climate change, and identity politics.

The concept of the cultural complex provided a new conceptualization of a level of experience and influence juxtaposed between the archetypal-collective level and the individual-personal level. The concept incorporates the idea that individual experience is shaped by the groups and cultures they are engaged with while also underscoring the idea that a group or cultural milieu can be contaminated or impacted emotionally, behaviorally, and perceptually by attitudes or perceptions emerging within a group or culture.

Cultural complexes are akin to personal complexes that when activated take hold of the collective psyche of the group. At times, cultural complexes may also function as a part of traumatic group defense. Naturally, we have seen numerous examples of active cultural complexes playing out across the world during recent years. However, cultural complexes also have adaptive functions as well, such as organizing group life, facilitating the functioning of the individual within the group, and providing a sense of belonging.

Complexes: Parallels with Other Psychoanalytic Schools

Clearly, there are significant parallels between complex theory and object relations theory. Plaut (1974, 1975), Redfearn (1985, 1994), Field (1994), Charlton (1997), Knox (1997), and Solomon (1991) all highlight the similarities (and some differences) between complex theory and object relations theory. Object relations theory is an outgrowth of the theoretical model of Melanie Klein. Object relations is an inclusive technical term that spans the intrapsychic and interpersonal dimensions. According to Scharff and Scharff, "An internal object is a piece of psychic structure that formed from the person's experience with the important caretaking person in earlier life, captured as a trace of that earlier relationship" (1992, p. 5). An internal object relation,

> refers to the system of in-built parts of the personality in relationship to each other inside the self. ... Internal objects and other parts of the self are reciprocal with outer parts so that, in any relationship, the personalities are mutually influenced by each other. Our external relationships are in interaction with our internal psychic structures.
>
> (1992, p. 4)

Complex theory and object relations theory both describe internal representational structures of the psyche which shape perception, response, and action. As Redfearn (1985) points out, while complexes often reflect an internalization of early object relations, a main conceptual difference between complex theory and object relations theory is that complexes are also frequently organized around themes, things, or situations, such as inferiority, money, sexuality, power, victimization, intimacy, success, failure, or avoidance. Redfearn (1985, p. xiii) refers collectively to complexes, internalized objects and part-objects, and elements of body image as 'sub-personalities' that contribute to the making of our 'many selves.' However, other schools of thought also have similar constructs used to explain, understand, and illustrate centers of psychological structure within the unconscious, utilizing terms such as affect-laden thematic organizations, image schemas, representations of interactions generalized (RIGs), internal working models, narrative scripts, personal constructs, and pathogenic adaptations.

Personally, I conceptualize psychological structure through a hybrid of complex theory and object relations theory. I find there are benefits to both theories and limitations to both theories. I find complex theory to be a more flexible, adaptable theory which can be applied to a wider variety of situations and themes than the conceptual language of object relations. However, it is more difficult to speak about complexes in a dynamic, interactive manner. Jung frequently refers to complexes as being projected onto outer relationships and indicates that the therapeutic task is to facilitate the withdrawal of the patient's projections so that the elements of the complexes being projected become available for integration into the patient's personality. In contrast, object relations theory more readily captures the dynamic relationships, i.e., between the patient's ego, internal object relationships, and outer object relationships. Additionally, object relations theory captures the variation in the stability of internal object relations, e.g., object constancy, which is not present in complex theory. As a result, I tend to utilize elements of both complex theory and object relations theory, appreciating the flexibility of focus found in complex theory and the interactive, dynamic application of object relations theory.

Critique/Assessment of Complex Theory

As mentioned earlier there has been considerable criticism and debate around Jung's theory of the anima/animus complex. There has been far less general critique, assessment, or reappraisal of Jung's theory of complexes than there has been for his theory of archetypes and the collective unconscious. In my opinion, Bovensiepen's article (2006) outlining a contemporary perspective on complex theory with an emphasis on an interactive network of complexes is the most valuable revisioning of complex theory in the Jungian literature.

The other available contemporary commentaries on complex theory primarily offer confirmatory support for Jung's theory of complexes. Escamilla et al. sought to empirically "validate the theory of complexes and elucidate the neuropsychologic mechanisms underlying the unconscious activation of significant memories" (2018, p. 484) by administering the WAT to a group of subjects while monitoring their brain function using functional magnetic resonance imaging (fMRI). Using this technology, the researchers were able to "observe distinct differences in brain reaction when a person is responding to complex triggering words in comparison to neutral words" (2018, p. 486). Escamilla et al. concluded that their findings, in terms of the patterns of brain activation during the administration of WAT, fit remarkably well with Jung's theory of complexes, particularly the idea that each complex manifests through three primary modes of experience: "a bodily component, a language and symbol component, and an affective component" (2018, p. 503).

Roesler and van Uffelen (2018) review research from cognitive psychology and the neurosciences that supports or implies the existence of a dynamic unconscious and complexes, as well as contemporary research on the WAT and dissociative identity disorder. In addition, they carried out their own research program comparing the results of the WAT with standardized diagnostic measures. They concluded that all the symptoms and problem areas identified by standardized diagnostic measures could also be identified with the WAT, thus providing contemporary empirical support for Jung's theory of complexes.

An article by Krieger (2019) covers similar territory, reviewing the available neuroscience research with the WAT. However, Krieger also interprets the available research through dynamic systems theory and identifies a three-part model of complex activation centered on the cyclical interaction of three primary states, the first state being the initial activation of perception, instinct, and emotion. This is followed within milliseconds by state two – activation of somatic reaction, awareness, and memory. State three involves the emergence of potentially symbolic images and therefore meaning. Ultimately, she concludes, "One of the points these studies have underlined is the change in awareness brought on by the constellation, and even the activation, of a complex" (2019, p. 756).

One issue that can be raised about complex theory and its clinical application, particularly among those practicing from a classical Jungian perspective, is the emphasis placed on encouraging the patient to identify and withdraw their projections from others so that the material being projected onto another person becomes available for integration into the personality of the person engaging in the projection. This emphasis is especially pronounced around the shadow and anima/animus complexes and is found throughout Jung's writings, for example:

> But if, as the result of a long and thorough analysis and the withdrawal of projections, the ego has been successfully separated from the unconscious, the anima will gradually cease to act as an autonomous personality and will become a function of relationship between conscious and unconscious. So long as she is projected, she leads to all sorts of illusions about people and things and thus to endless complications. The withdrawal of projections makes the anima what she originally was: an archetypal image which, in its right place, functions to the advantage of the individual.
>
> (1954/1966, ¶504)

However, many patients seek analysis without having developed an adequate symbolic capacity or their symbolic capacity has been disrupted by trauma. These patients largely function on the concrete level. Individuals functioning at the concrete level interpret their perceptions as facts and their capacity to reflect on their perceptions as subjective or from an 'as if' perspective is limited. Put most simply, concrete thinking is "a failure to symbolize and differentiate" (Tuch 2011, p. 770). That is, to differentiate self from other, inner from outer, conscious from unconscious, real from imagined. As Tuch puts it:

> Failure to discriminate symbol from symbolized is the essence of concrete thinking. The concrete thinker lacks access to differentiated symbols with which to take a metaphoric leap away from tight adherence to concrete reality in order then to reapproach the matter from a different angle.
>
> (2011, p. 773)

Because the withdrawal of projections involves a degree of symbolic capacity which many patients lack, I have argued that this emphasis on the withdrawal of projections emphasized in the classical Jungian framework is most often ineffectual and sometimes damaging to the analytic process with patients functioning at the concrete level. With patients who have limited symbolic capacity:

> We should avoid interpretations which are intended to facilitate the withdrawal of the patient's projection onto another person. Projections cannot be withdrawn without some capacity for symbolic function because the withdrawal of a projection involves being capable of experiencing their perceptions as subjective rather than factual.
>
> (Winborn 2023, p. 98)

Note

1 Bovensiepen (2006) discusses the defense organization of complexes (p. 453) as well as referring to similar material in Knox (2003).

Suggestions for Further Reading

Classic Papers

Jung, C.G. (1911). On the doctrine of complexes. In *CW2*. Princeton, NJ: Princeton University Press.

Jung, C.G. (1948b). A review of the complex theory. In *CW8*. Princeton, NJ: Princeton University Press.

Additional Reading

Bovensiepen, G. (2006). Attachment-dissociation network: Some thoughts about a modern complex theory. *J. Anal. Psychol.*, *51*: 451–466.

Dieckmann, H. (1999). *Complexes: Diagnosis and Therapy in Analytical Psychology.* Wilmette, IL: Chiron.

Shalit, E. (2002). *The Complex: Path of Transformation from Archetype to Ego.* Toronto: Inner City Books.

Chapter 5

Jungian Perspectives on Dreams

Dreams hold a place of prominence within Jungian psychoanalysis and in the curricula of Jungian training programs. Many individuals drawn to practice as Jungian psychoanalysts are initially attracted by the special emphasis Jung placed on dreams. As mentioned earlier, following his split with Freud, Jung began to outline out his model of the psyche, contrasting it with Freud's model. Jung's model of dreaming was laid out as a repudiation of Freud's model and as a repudiation of many elements of Freud's model of psychic functioning in general. Because of this, despite the many changes in contemporary psychoanalysis since Freud's death, it remains relevant to discuss Jung's model of dreaming in contrast to Freud's model.

Jung did not believe the origins of dream content could be solely reduced to infantile, forgotten, or repressed wishes. Following their split, Jung promptly abandoned Freud's conceptualization of the dream as possessing both manifest and latent contents. Unlike Freud, Jung did not conceive the dream as having a hidden meaning which was disguised to protect the sleep of the dreamer from distressing contents entering the dream unfiltered. Therefore, Jung's theory of dreaming had no place for a distorting censor which undermined Freud's fundamental concept of dreamwork, i.e., the distortion process which transforms the hidden latent content of the dream into the manifest content, i.e., the dream as remembered. For Jung, the meaning of a dream was not difficult to understand because of the distorting-disguising effects of the dreamer's defenses but because the conscious state of the dreamer

DOI: 10.4324/9781003223511-6

is not oriented to understanding the symbolic-metaphorical language which dreams speak in. In other words, dreams could be understood if we more fully grasped the language of metaphor and symbol through which dreams are communicated. Interestingly, self psychology, as developed by Heinz Kohut, modifies Freud's dream theory by placing greater emphasis on the manifest content of a dream, which Kohut conceptualized as communicating the state of the dreamer's self, i.e., self-state dreams (Mitchell and Black 1995, p. 261 fn5).

While Jung did retain some of the defense mechanisms from Freud's model, i.e., condensation, displacement, and symbolization as aspects of dream formation, he no longer associated these processes with the concept of a dream censor which distorts the latent content of the dream into the more tolerable manifest content. Instead, he saw these processes as part of the process by which dream symbols are generated. Additionally, Jung saw dreams as an avenue to understanding the composition and function of the complexes within the overall structure of the unconscious, an understanding which was much more important to him than the goal of uncovering past events.

Jung assumed the dream was a direct psychological statement, a self-portrayal, of the unconscious situation of the dreamer, e.g., "The dream is a spontaneous self-portrayal, in symbolic form, of the actual situation in the unconscious" (1916/1948, ¶505). This is a point he continues to make throughout his writing, e.g., "The dream comes in as the expression of an involuntary, unconscious psychic process beyond the control of the conscious mind. It shows the inner truth and reality of the patient as it is really not as I conjecture it to be, and not as he would like it to be, but as it is" (1931/1934, ¶304).

This view of dream as self-portrayal was complemented by Jung's proposal about the compensatory function of the dream. For Jung, one of the primary functions of the dream was to assist in the self-regulating system of the psyche, i.e., "Dreams are the natural reaction of the self-regulating psychic system" (1935, ¶248) and he saw dreams as symptoms of a self-regulating internal process, "They [dreams] are an indication, a symptom … that the individual is at variance with unconscious conditions, that somewhere he has deviated from his natural path" (1935, ¶247).

Jung saw this self-regulation as taking place largely through the process of compensation, i.e., the unconscious seeking to balance or 'compensate' for a one-sided, unbalanced attitude in the dreamer's conscious perspective, e.g., "Dreams I maintain are compensatory to the conscious situation of the moment" (1916/1948, ¶487), and asking, "What conscious attitude does it [the dream] compensate?" (1931/1934, ¶334). Elaborating further, Jung goes on to state, "The concept of compensation seemed to me the only adequate one, for it alone is capable of summing up all the various ways in which a dream behaves. … Compensation on the other hand, as the term implies, means balancing and comparing different data or points of view so as to produce an adjustment or a rectification" (1945/1948, ¶545).

Jung also conceptualized dreams as having a teleological function, i.e., guiding the dreamer towards some not yet realized state of being. He sometimes referred to this as the finalistic or prospective function of dreaming, e.g., "Considering a dream from a standpoint of finality … does not involve a denial of the dream's causes but rather a different interpretation of the associative material gathered round the dream" (1916/1948, ¶462), and "The dream … would then have the value of a positive, guiding idea or of an aim whose vital meaning would be greatly superior to that of the momentarily constellated conscious content" (1916/1948, ¶491). Jung attributed the origin of this guiding aim to the Self.

Grotstein, working from a Kleinian/Bionian perspective, has offered a conceptualization that is similar to Jung's concept of the relationship between the Self, the dream, and the dream ego. Grotstein conceptualizes the dynamic as the 'Dreamer Who Dreams the Dream' (the aspect of the psyche generating/creating the dream) and the 'Dreamer Who Understands the Dream' (the aspect of the psyche receiving and responding to the dream) (2000, pp. 5–15). Grotstein describes the dynamic of this relationship as follows, "Ultimately, the Dreamer Who Dreams the Dream is the Ineffable Subject of Being who registers catastrophic changes and transmits them as a dream narrative to the Dreamer Who Understands the Dream for corrective completion" (2000, p. 9). For Grotstein, 'Ineffable Subject of Being' refers to something that is unconscious, not known, numinous, and other, yet still retains some "sense of I-ness, which seeks its reflection in its self-ness" (2000, p. 11). Grotstein's description of the 'Dreamer Who Dreams the Dream' and the 'Ineffable Subject of Being' are quite close to Jung's description of the function and experience of the Self.

Jung's approach to working with dream was both phenomen-ological and hermeneutical. In other words, the patient's and analyst's experience of the dream is essential, "I would not give priority to understanding. … For the important thing is not to interpret and understand the fantasies, but primarily to experience them" (1966, ¶342). Elsewhere Jung underscores the experiential nature of dreams, stating, "we do not dream, but rather we *are dreamt*. We are the object of the dream, not its maker" (2008, p. 159, italics in original).

In terms of working with dreams, Jung observed that many dreams were similar in structure to ancient Greek plays (Jacobi 1973, p. 83, Jung 1945/1948, ¶561–564), with dreams frequently having characteristic structural elements: a context (i.e. place, time, and main characters – 'dramatis personae'), exposition (i.e., statement of the problem), plot development, a crisis or movement towards a climax (peripeteia), and a lysis (i.e., the solution or resolution of the dream, often containing the compensatory ele-ment of the dream in terms of the conscious situation). Classical Jungian dreamwork typically involves four elements: 1) the patient's retelling of the dream; 2) gathering the patient's associa-tions to the various dream elements as well as the day residues preceding the dream; 3) providing amplifications from the ana-lyst's knowledge of archetypal themes, often involving elements drawn from myths, fairy tales, religious motifs, or alchemical motifs, however, amplifications might also be offered from current events, literature, poetry, music, film, or other sources; 4) an interpretation of the dream, ideally co-created by the analyst and patient.

From Jung's perspective, the amplification process was essential, feeling that the dream was embedded not only in personal experi-ence but universal or collective aspects of experience, "In analy-tical psychology, we resort to amplification in the interpretation of dreams, for a dream is too slender a hint to be understood until it is enriched by the stuff of association and analogy and thus amplified to the point of intelligibility" (1968, ¶403). Jung describes this process as hermeneutical in approach:

> The essence of hermeneutics … consists in adding further analogies to the one already supplied by the symbol: in the first place, subjective analogies produced at random by the patient, then objective analogies provided by the analyst out of his general knowledge. This procedure widens and enriches the initial symbol, and the final outcome is an infinitely complex and variegated picture. … Certain lines of psychological development then stand out that are at once individual and collective.
>
> (1916/1928, ¶493)

In terms of the amplifications drawn from archetypal sources, the aim is to identify a few central motifs or stories that capture a psychological 'truth' or essence of the patient's psychological situation on which the analysis becomes centered for a period of time, perhaps even utilized as a metaphorical touchstone for the remainder of the analysis.

For Jung, the goal of dreamwork and dream interpretation was to assist the patient in assimilating the symbolic contents of the dream into the conscious perspective of the dreamer, thus enlarging the field of consciousness, "Through the assimilation of unconscious contents [dreams], the momentary life of consciousness can once more be brought into harmony with the law of nature from which it all too easily departs, and the patient can be led back to the natural law of his own being" (1931/1934, ¶351). According to Jung, each individual's task is, ultimately, "to become conscious of the contents that press upward from the unconscious. … As far as we can discern the sole purpose of human existence is to kindle a light in the darkness of mere being" (1965, p. 326).

Developments in Jungian Dream Approaches

The 'classical' Jungian approach to dreams remains the most widely taught and applied theory/method of dreamwork within analytical psychology. As mentioned in Chapter 1, there have been three primary orientations which emerged within analytical psychology, with each orientation developing different points of emphasis or approach. For example, the developmental school de-emphasizes the importance of archetypal amplification while emphasizing the representation of early developmental disruptions and the transference–countertransference matrix as they appear in dreams.

Hillman and those from the archetypal orientation focus less on dream interpretation, gathering associations, or amplification. While the archetypal approach takes its initial inspiration from Jung, it also has roots in Greek philosophy, phenomenology, renaissance humanism, and existentialism. Their emphasis is on deepening the dreamer's experience of the images appearing in the dream, a process they refer to as 'soul-making.' In his approach to dreams, Hillman encourages the analyst and patient to 'stick to the image,' i.e., focus on the subjective experience of a dream or fantasy image. This was a central focus of his book *The Dream and the Underworld* (1979a) wherein he makes a distinction between 'day world' interpretations (which translate the image) and 'night world' interpretations (which deepen the experience of the image). Hillman believed that 'day world' interpretations, often influenced more by the analyst's knowledge of patient's history and use of theory, are too influenced by the ego awareness/ concerns of the analyst. Many characteristics of the archetypal school's approach to dreams can be found in Hillman (1977, 1978, 1979a, 1979b) and Berry (1982). I see the archetypal approach as more of a philosophy or stance taken in relationship with the patient's dreams, rather than the application of a specific method.

The archetypal approach encourages the dreamer and the ana-lyst to deepen the experience of dream imagery through sensory engagement with the dream (e.g., smells, textures, color, tempera-ture, sounds), as well as the emotions reflected in the dream, the interconnectedness of images within the dream, relative positions of figures and objects in the dream, and the overall narrative. Hillman indicates that at least two senses must be engaged to develop a sense of an image. The archetypal school also attempts to conceive of the entire dream as occurring simultaneously, with no preference given to images appearing earlier or later in the dream, as is often encountered with the approach of the classical school.

While amplification is still utilized, there is greater emphasis within the archetypal school on ensuring all amplifications maintain an essential correspondence with the dream image rather than introducing amplifications which potentially lead away from the original dream image. From the archetypal perspective, the analyst also attends to repetitions within the dream – such as repetition of similar figures, actions, situations, themes, or adjectives. Ultimately, sensitivity to these qualities of the dream images deepens the metaphoric action of the image and therefore the experience of 'soul.'

As mentioned above, in archetypal psychology, there is also a movement away from formal interpretation, towards 'word play.' Hillman argued that our usual patterns of speech often keep the dreamer and the analyst away from 'hearing' what the image is saying. Hillman encourages the analyst to break down the literalism in ordinary speech, e.g., by turning nouns found in dreams into adjectives, utilizing puns, and reversing word order (e.g., 'hurry desperately' becomes 'despair hurriedly').

Another approach has been outlined by Robert Bosnak in *Tracks in the Wilderness of Dreaming* (1986). Bosnak focuses his attention, and the patient's attention, on the atmospheric, sensory, and affective qualities of the dream, i.e., the phenomenological experience inside the dream rather than the 'meaning' of the dream. He advocates attempting to subjectively identify the emotional nodal center of the dream and to circumambulate around that center, in an attempt to deepen the patient's sensory-affective-somatic response to the dream without moving too quickly to the stages of amplification and interpretation. Clearly, there are some similarities between Bosnak's approach and the approach of the archetypal school. However, Bosnak's approach does not have the same philosophical emphasis on dreaming as 'soul-making,' nor does he elevate 'image' to the same level of significance. Bosnak is more focused on the patient's emerging experience of the dream than on 'sticking with the image' or on 'soul-making.'

I find Bosnak's approach more effective than the classical approach when dreams are brought into sessions by patients functioning at the concrete level (Winborn 2023). With patients who have limited symbolic capacity I avoid engaging in a classical stepwise Jungian approach to dreamwork, i.e., inquiring about the residue of the day, gathering associations, offering archetypal amplifications, attempting to understand the dramatic structure of the dream, and attempting to create a collaborative interpretation of the dream. While Bosnak did not develop his approach in order to address the analytic situation with concrete patients, it none-theless works well with concrete patients because the process does not require the patient to relate to the dream in a symbolic manner, nor does it require them to understand the various ele-ments represented in the dream from a perspective outside their own concrete orientation. For example, if someone functioning concretely brings a dream in which they were frozen, I would not ask them for their associations to frozenness, offer archetypal amplifications around the theme of frozenness, or make a histori-cally based interpretation like, "I think your emotions feel frozen because you felt they were rejected by your parents while you were growing up and you felt you needed to freeze them in order to prevent them from being damaged further." Instead, I would begin by simply inquiring, "What was it like for you being frozen?" This allows the patient to 'engage' or 'approach' poten-tially symbolic material without having to defend their under-standing of a dream element. With patients functioning at the concrete level, if I offer an amplification, it is typically drawn from film, television, novels, or something occurring in the patient's immediate cultural milieu. Amplifications from these sources still have the benefit of introducing metaphorical interaction but are more readily assimilated by the patient.

Finally, West (2011) offers a post-Jungian approach to dreams. In a refreshingly open manner, he presents the psychoanalytic perspective and Jungian perspectives as necessarily existing side-by-side without disparaging or championing the desirability or correctness of one over the other. West does not present a restate-ment of the classical Jungian perspective on dreams; rather he offers a well-developed evolution of the Jungian model, updated, and expanded with insights from a variety of sources, including contemporary dream research, infant observation, developmental theory, neurosciences, and his own original perspectives. Ultimately, the incorporation of this material from other fields offers additional evidence for the value of dreamwork, extending beyond accumulated clinical experience, for a variety of analytic theories. West carefully selects the material from these related fields to underscore the interwoven relationship between the central psychological activities of association, symbolization, and emotion. One of West's unique contributions is his focus on early childhood experiences (patterns) in dream formation. Also fertile is his consideration of the dream as supervisor to the therapist or analyst.

Jungian and Bionian Dreamwork

In my own practice, I have found the work of Wilfred Bion and various post-Bionian authors provide the most valuable complement to and expansion of my clinical approach to dreams. The function of dreamwork for both Bion and Jung shifts away from the classical dream model of Freud in which the analyst's task is to translate from the manifest content of the dream into the latent content of the dream, revealing the underlying wish, feeling, or fantasy that is threatening to the ego of the analysand. Just as Jung did, Wilfred Bion, Antonino Ferro, Donald Meltzer, and Giuseppe Civitarese all emphasize the constructive, purposive aspects of the dream as well as holding a primary focus on the manifest qualities of the dream. As Civitarese puts it, "the manifest text is already the expression of a completed process of symbolization" (2015, p. 48). For Jung, the dream speaks for itself and reveals its meaning in the language of symbols (often communicated in images), not to obscure, but because symbols are expressed in the language of the unconscious. In Jung's model, dreams also function to facilitate the creation of the personality, "Every dream is an organ of information and control, and why dreams are our most effective aid in building up the personality" (1954/1966, ¶332).

Like Jung, Bion began with Freud's notion of 'dreamwork' and broadened its meaning, expanding it to encompass disparate phenomena ranging from the normal to the extremely pathological. Freud's idea of dreams serving the pleasure principle remained intact, but Bion (1983) provided an understanding of how dreams could also be in service of the reality principle by giving representation to raw emotional experience. The dream portrays the emotional state of the dreamer, and it is incumbent on the dreamer and the analyst to comprehend the emotional state being presented. In the Bionian model, dreaming is seen as occurring in both waking states and sleeping states; there is no distinction between waking and sleeping in terms of dreaming. In waking states, the conscious mind is not aware of dreaming, but the individual continues their unconscious efforts to dream themselves into existence. Jung also hypothesized the possibility of waking dreams, "It is on the whole probable that we continually dream but that consciousness makes such a noise that we do not hear it" (quoted in Jacobi 1973, p. 73).

Dreaming in Bion's model refers to unconscious psychological work that someone does with their emotional experiences. It is through this work that we attempt to dream ourselves into being. We have no direct experience of the waking dream; we can only recognize it through the behavioral and narrative derivatives that filter into our conscious thoughts and actions. Listening from Bion's perspective is not just listening that is filtered through a different set of theoretical constructs; it is listening in a different way, just as listening for the archetypal layer in the Jungian framework is a different way of listening than other psychoanalytic models. In Bion's model of dreaming, the emphasis shifts away from the meaning and symbolic content of dreams and refocuses our attention onto the process of dreaming as an experience (or non-experience) of being. Note the teleological parallel between Jung's model of individuation and Bion's idea of 'dreaming ourselves into existence.' Bion's model of dreaming builds a bridge which allows a Jungian perspective on dreams to coexist with a psychoanalytic perspective on dreaming (Winborn 2018).

In Bion's model, the work of analysis still involves the work of understanding symbolic content, which reveals unconscious meanings, but analysis also becomes a process of metabolizing unsymbolized aspects of experience which have never been conscious and never been repressed because they've never risen to the level of a thought. Only by working on this level can those experiences become available for reflection and symbol production. This element of Bion's model articulates a level of experience which is only alluded to in passing in Jung's model. In Bion's model, the focus shifts to the qualities of a patient's patterns of speech – alive or impoverished, the way the patient inhabits their body, the specificity of their feeling states, or the level of differentiation of their experiences. Shifts in these qualities point to an increased capacity to digest or metabolize experience and ultimately to greater coherence of Self. Bion relies on four concepts to outline the process of the transformation from un-represented, un-symbolized experience into psychological experience available for symbolic productions: beta elements, alpha function, alpha elements, and reverie (Winborn 2017).

Beta elements are raw bits of unmetabolized, undigested proto-experience which are precursory to sensory, psychic, affective, or somatic experience. These bits do not have meaning and are not sufficiently formed or coalesced to be reflected upon but will be utilized for projective identification, enactments, and overt actions. Because beta elements operate outside awareness and have not yet been represented, they are not available for thought, reflection, or learning and are not subject to repression or suppression.

Alpha elements are experiences which have become sufficiently coalesced to be reflected upon. They are produced from the impressions of experience which have been made storable and available for dream thoughts and for unconscious waking thinking. Alpha elements do not yet have meaning but are capable of being worked with as psychological events by an individual, somewhat analogous to the way in which words can be grouped together to form sentences and paragraphs which have narrative meaning. Alpha elements become building blocks of experience which have the potential to become connected together to form dream thoughts. For Bion, dream thoughts are the components of dreaming conceptualized as occurring both during sleeping and waking states unless the capacity to dream has been disrupted.

The alpha function refers to the capacity of the analyst to contain elements of their psyche and the patient's psyche while engaging in reverie about the patient's beta elements in order to facilitate their transformation into alpha elements. In order for the patient to learn from experience, the alpha function of the analyst must operate with an awareness of the proto-emotional experience of the patient until the patient develops sufficient alpha function to participate in the process as a mutually constellated alpha function. Interpretations generated from the analyst's alpha function are not intended to give the patient understanding or meaning per se, but rather to help the patient recognize these experiences, develop a language for describing and remembering them, and to facilitate the organization of previously unorganized experience.

The alpha function is similar to the transcendent function except in Jung's model the transcendent function operates to generate symbolic material and functions intrapsychically while in Bion's model the alpha function operates intersubjectively and on the level of the pre-representational. We can think of alpha function as operating on a more fundamental level of transformation than the transcendent function – the level of very small, almost imperceptible shifts which transform unintegrated elements of experience into usable bits of experience. These transformed bits become the building blocks of larger shifts involved with the symbolization process of the transcendent function and the capacity to individuate. It seems likely that the alpha function and the transcendent function of the analyst work in conjunction but are engaged with transforming different levels of experience. I recently became aware that Civitarese and Ferro (2013, p. 200) and Grotstein (2007, p. 271), have also conceptualized along similar lines, proposing an 'alpha-megafunction' operating on a similar level of experience as Jung's transcendent function. Bion's model and the concept of non-representational states expand our perspective on the general categories of experience which might be encountered in an analytic session: 1) symbolized, 2) non-symbolized/concrete, 3) repressed unconscious, and 4) non-represented/not repressed unconscious.

Reverie is the primary way of accessing, perceiving, experiencing, and working with the states and psychic elements outlined by Bion and analysts engaging non-representational experience. Reverie is opening to one's own internal stream of consciousness and unconscious promptings – opening to ideas, thoughts, feelings, sensations, memories, images, urges, and fantasies. Reverie involves being receptive on many levels to the experience and communication, both explicit and implicit, of the other person's presence in the room. It also includes sensitivity to the emerging analytic third in the reverie field.

In the post-Bionian model the dream becomes the vehicle to "develop the narrative competence of the mind. That's why we say working with dreams and not on dreams" (Civitarese 2015, p. xiii). Civitarese states, "the dream becomes the very model of thought" (2015, p. xiv). Civitarese indicates that "dream space" (a psychological 'space' in which dreaming can occur) is an acquired capacity, rather than existing as an innate capacity, which complements the Jungian concept of symbolic capacity, seeing it as an outcome of analysis rather than something required of the patient in order to undertake analysis, "Unlike dreaming as an innate psychic process, dream space belongs to the field of the symbolic and as a result is acquired over time" (2015, p. 84).

In my practice, another significant influence from the post-Bionian theory of dreaming is Ogden's (2017) concept of 'dreaming the analytic session.' Ogden proposes we hold each session as though it is a dream and wonder about what is appearing/happening in the session as though these elements being introduced are elements in a dream. I find this way of 'holding' the session facilitates listening and experiencing the session from a different 'vertex' (Bion 1965), i.e., the vertex of dreaming. I find I more readily read/hear 'between the lines' and sense implicit and symbolic communications when I am able to hold the session as a dream (Winborn 2022). Ogden indicates, "Each analyst must find his or her own way of dreaming each session with each patient. Dreaming the session is not something one works at; rather, one tries not to get in its way" (2017, p. 1).

In terms of dreamwork in analysis, the Bionian perspective also emphasizes the analyst's 'negative capability' (Bion 1970/1983), i.e., Bion's term for the analyst's capacity to tolerate uncertainty and not knowing. For many Jungians, cultivating 'negative capability' often will take the form of moving beyond the urge to conceptualize material emerging in sessions in terms of the familiar structures of complexes or archetypal patterns, while leaving room for other possibilities to emerge through reverie. Also of significance is the Bionian perspective that there is a level of experience we are always moving towards but never fully know (i. e., the thing in itself), just as Jung describes the experience of the archetype in a similar way, as something experienced but not fully known. Bion refers to this level of experience as "O" – which he generally defines as the ineffable transcendent aspect of experience.

The Bionian concepts outlined above have allowed me to build upon my Jungian foundation of dreamwork – complementing, enriching, and expanding my approach to dreams. In working with dreams, I focus less on attempting to understand the meaning of a dream, focus more on trying to understand how the dream is facilitating the metabolization of experience.

Research and Jungian Dream Theory

Recently, there has been an increase in research on Jungian dream theory. Utilizing a research methodology called 'structural dream analysis' (SDA), Roesler (2020) evaluated the dreams produced by patients in Jungian -oriented therapy. SDA allows for systematic and objective analysis of the meaning of dreams produced by patients. The method focuses especially on the relationship between the dream ego and other figures in the dream and the extent of activity of the dream ego. In Roesler's research project, five major dream patterns were identified which accounted for the majority of the dreams. The subjects' dream series were typically dominated by one or two repetitive patterns which reflected the psychological issues of the dreamers. Additionally, typical changes in the dream series' patterns could be identified which corresponded with therapeutic change. According to Roesler, "the findings support Jung's theory of dreams as providing a holistic image of the dreamer's psyche, including unconscious aspects" (2020, p. 44).

In another research project, Vedfelt (2020) integrates findings from neuroscience, empirical dream research, and complex cybernetic information networks that provide support for many of the basic tenets of Jung's theory of dreaming. He indicates that his research and analysis identify ten core qualities of dreams which also are applicable to understanding dreams in clinical practice:

1) Dreams deal with matters important to us; 2) Dreams symbolize; 3) Dreams personify; 4) Dreams are trial runs in a safe place; 5) Dreams are online to unconscious intelligence; 6) Dreams are pattern recognition; 7) Dreams are high level

communication; 8) Dreams are condensed information; 9) Dreams are experiences of wholeness; 10) Dreams are psychological energy landscapes.

(2020, p. 88)

Suggestions for Further Reading

Classic Papers

Jung, C.G. (1916/1948). General aspects of dream psychology. In *CW8*. Princeton, NJ: Princeton University Press.

Jung, C.G. (1931/1934). The practical use of dream-analysis. In *CW16*. Princeton, NY: Princeton University Press.

Jung, C.G. (1945/1948). On the nature of dreams. In *CW8*. Princeton, NJ: Princeton University Press.

Additional Reading

Bosnak, R. (1986). *Tracks in the Wilderness of Dreaming*. New York: Delacorte Press.

Civitarese, G. (2015). *The Necessary Dream: New Theories and Techniques of Interpretation in Psychoanalysis*. London: Karnac.

Hillman, J. (1979). *The Dream and the Underworld*. New York: Harper & Row.

West, M. (2011). *Understanding Dreams in Clinical Practice*. London: Karnac.

Whitmont, E. and Perera, S.B. (1989). *Dreams: A Portal to the Source*. London: Routledge.

Chapter 6

Other Key Concepts in Jungian Psychoanalysis

Processes, States, and Energy

Libido

As mentioned in Chapter 1, differences with Freud over the conceptualization of libido were one of the primary causes of their split. Jung felt Freud's concept of libido, founded mainly on concrete phenomena such as aggressive or sexual drives, did not adequately depict the dynamic changes he observed in terms of shifts in libido. For Jung, Freud's libido theory failed to differentiate vital energy from psychic energy. Jung proposed that libido was a life energy thereby conceptualizing libido as having a wider scope that encompassed psychic as well as biological energy. As Jacobi puts it, "Libido or psychic energy in the Jungian sense is the foundation and regulator of all psychic life" (1973, p. 59). Jacobi goes on to describe the breadth of Jung's conceptualization of libido:

> By psychic energy he means the total force which pulses through all the forms and activities of the psychic system and establishes a communication between them. He calls this kind of psychic energy libido. It is nothing other than the intensity of the psychic process, its psychological value, which can be determined only by psychic manifestations and effects. … In other words, energy is always experienced specifically as motion and force when actual and as a state or condition potential. When actualized, psychic energy is reflected in the specific phenomena of the psyche: drives, wishes, will, affect,

DOI: 10.4324/9781003223511-7

performance, and the like. But when it is only potential, it is manifested in specific acquisitions, possibilities, aptitudes, and attitudes, etc.

(1973, pp. 52–53)

For Jung, libido originates from archetypal/instinctual forces which intensify the affective charge associated with activated complexes. When two opposite poles (e.g., conscious and unconscious, maternal and paternal, or masculine and feminine) are consciously held in dynamic tension (which Jung[1] refers to as the "tension of opposites"),[2] libido is channeled ("canalized") via the transcendent function,[3] which in turn generates symbols[4] that carry the potential to heal and transform one-sided or maladaptive psychic positions, structures, and attitudes into new configurations, with the ultimate aim being individuation[5] (Jung 1948c, 1958).

In terms of the movement of libido, Jung attended to the progression and regression of libido within the patient's psychological system, something he indicated could be observed in dreams, fantasies, symptoms, affects, and behavioral patterns. He saw progression and regression as "transitional stages in the flow of energy" (Jung 1948c, ¶76). Jung contrasted regressive movement of energy (back towards an earlier state of organization) with progressive movement (towards a new state of psychological configuration). He described progression as a "continuous process of adaptation to environmental conditions" (Jung 1948c, ¶74). However, Jung did not see regression in a negative light. He proposed that unconscious contents are activated during regression and therefore regression often is necessary for new psychological growth. Jung indicated that regression occurs when there is a blockage of forward movement of energy due to the inability of the dominant conscious attitude to adapt to changing circumstances:

> Regression, on the other hand, as an adaptation to the conditions of the inner world, springs from the vital need to satisfy the demands of individuation. … He can meet the demands of outer necessity in an ideal way only if he is also adapted to his own inner world, that is if he is in harmony

with himself. Conversely, he can only adapt to his inner world and achieve harmony with himself when he is adapted to the environmental conditions.

(Jung 1948c, ¶75)

Jung's most fully developed position on libido is found in his paper "On Psychic Energy" (1948c).

Symbol

Symbolic capacity is at the very core of C.G. Jung's analytical psychology. The ability to relate to myth, image, symbol, and the imaginal realm are all dependent on the notion of symbolization and the patient's symbolic capacity. Jung indicates the psyche is mythopoetic, meaning that the psyche creates personal myths which are symbolic metaphors for ways of being, understanding, experiencing. Symbols originate from an in-between place, a place between body and spirit, and therefore have the capacity to engage and integrate, not only feeling and thought but also soul. Symbols allow us to see, feel, and speak about a living connection between elements of experience and form the building blocks for transformation and the unfolding of the individuation process.

Jung described Freud's use of symbols as "an abbreviated designation for a known thing" (Jung 1971, ¶815). For Jung the symbol always referred to a spontaneous attempt of the unconscious to express in known images something relatively unknown:

An expression that stands for a known thing remains a mere sign and is never a symbol. It is, therefore, quite impossible to create a living symbol, i.e., one that is pregnant with meaning, from known associations. … Every psychic product, if it is the best possible expression at the moment for a fact as yet unknown or only relatively known, may be regarded as a symbol, provided that we accept the expression as standing for something that is only divined and not yet clearly conscious.

(Jung 1971, ¶817)

Elsewhere, Jung indicates that a symbol is "the best possible expression of a complex fact not yet clearly apprehended by consciousness" (Jung 1958, ¶148).

All symbols begin as images of some kind, not just visual images, but also acoustic, somatic, olfactory, or kinesthetic symbols. Not all images that we experience become symbols, rather images exist as potential symbols. Jung emphasizes the unconscious origin of symbols, "Symbols were never devised consciously, but were always produced out of the unconscious by way of revelation or intuition" (1948c, ¶92), but also indicates that the individual's conscious attitude will determine whether an image becomes a living symbol, "Whether a thing is a symbol or not depends chiefly on the attitude of the observing consciousness" (Jung 1971, ¶818).

Clearly, from Jung's perspective, there must be a receptive conscious capacity present in the patient for an image to become a living symbol. The symbolic attitude is the phrase Jung uses to describe someone with the capacity for symbolic process. He describes the symbolic attitude as follows:

> The attitude that takes a given phenomenon as symbolic may be called ... the *symbolic attitude*. It is only partially justified by the behaviour of things; for the rest, it is the outcome of a definite view of the world which assigns meaning to events, and attaches to this meaning a greater value than to bare facts.
>
> (Jung 1971, ¶819)

Jung's concept of psychic reality is closely connected with establishing and maintaining a symbolic reality. The principle most central to the maintenance of an analytic attitude is Jung's concept of psychic reality. Jung defines psychic reality as follows:

> If I shift my concept of reality on to the plane of the psyche – where alone it is valid – this puts an end to the conflict between mind and matter, spirit and nature, as contradictory explanatory principles ... all immediate experience is psychic and that immediate reality can only be psychic. ... We could

well point to the idea of psychic reality as the most important achievement of modern psychology.

(Jung 1960/1969, ¶681–683)

The essential nature of psychic reality for the analytic process is also recognized by analysts from other psychoanalytic perspectives, for example Quinodoz, "The psychoanalyst is convinced of the presence and psychic reality of this world that transcends the limits of the measurable or the quantifiable" (2003, p. 134).

Jung also emphasizes the role of symbol in the conversion of psychic energy, "I have called a symbol that converts energy a '*libido analogue.*' By this I mean an idea that can give equivalent expression to the libido and canalize it into a form different from the original one" (Jung 1948c, ¶92). Solomon provides a fuller explanation of this process, describing symbols as,

> a bridge between complex and archetype. … The psychic manifestations of this generalised energy (libido) take the form of images (archetypal images), and these in turn become symbols when they act as transformers of energy, eventually offering the possibility of new resolutions of old problems.
>
> (1991, p. 312)

Transcendent Function

The transcendent function is a psychological function that arises from the tension between consciousness and the unconscious and supports the union of opposites. It expresses itself via the symbol and facilitates a transition from one psychological attitude or condition to another. In Jung's model, the transcendent function is the primary process by which individuation of the patient occurs. Jung describes the transcendent function as follows:

> The process of coming to terms with the unconscious is a true labour, a work which involves both action and suffering. It has been named the "transcendent function" because it represents a function based on real and "imaginary," or

rational and irrational, data, thus bridging the yawning gulf between conscious and unconscious. It is a natural process, a manifestation of the energy that springs from the tension of opposites.

(Jung 1917, ¶121)

The shuttling to and fro of arguments and affects represents the transcendent function of opposites. The confrontation of the two positions generates a tension charged with energy and creates a living third thing ... a movement out of the suspension between opposites, a living birth that leads to a new level of being, a new situation. The transcendent function manifests itself as a quality of conjoined opposites.

(Jung 1958, ¶189)

Jung's description of a 'living third thing' anticipates Ogden's (2004) concept of the 'analytic third.' Ogden conceptualizes along similar lines but makes a transition from the intrapsychic to the intersubjective, "the author conceives of projective identification as a form of the analytic third in which the individual subjectivities of analyst and analysand are subjugated to a co-created third subject of analysis" (2004, p. 167).

There are clear parallels between Jung's interwoven concepts of symbol, transcendent function, and the tension of opposites and Hegel's dialectical method in which he postulates that progress originates from a primary thesis proposition, a negation of that thesis (the antithesis), and a synthesis whereby the two conflicting ideas are reconciled to form a new proposition.

Jung's concept of the transcendent function also has similarities with Bion's concept of the alpha function. The alpha function is the psychological process by which beta elements become transformed into alpha elements. Bion proposes that there are levels of experience which have never been conscious and never been repressed because they've never risen to the level of a 'thought.' These are raw, unmetabolized bits of proto-experience which are largely somatic, sensory, or affective which Bion refers to as beta elements. Alpha elements are experiences which have become sufficiently coalesced to be reflected upon and become incorporated with other meaningful experience. Initially, the alpha function of the analyst facilitates the transformation of beta elements into alpha elements, but ultimately the goal is for the alpha function of the patient to become sufficiently developed to participate in the processing of experience.

The alpha function is similar to the transcendent function except in Jung's model the transcendent function operates to generate symbolic material and functions intrapsychically while in Bion's model the alpha function operates intersubjectively and on the level of the pre-representational. We can think of alpha function as operating on a more fundamental level of transformation than the transcendent function – the level of very small, almost imperceptible shifts which transform unintegrated elements of experience into usable bits of experience. These transformed bits become the building blocks of larger shifts involved with the symbolization process of the transcendent function and the capacity to individuate. It seems likely that the alpha function and the transcendent function of the analyst work in conjunction but are engaged with transforming different levels of experience. A fuller description of Bion's model of the psyche can be found in Chapter 5.

Typology

Following his split with Freud, Jung developed a theory of personality types to understand the fundamental differences between himself, Freud, and Alfred Adler, particularly in terms of how they arrived at different conclusions regarding the same psychological phenomenon. In addition to his experiences with Freud and Adler, Jung also based his model of typology on observations of his analysands and examination of trends in history, literature, philosophy, poetry, biography, religion, and aesthetics. His main ideas regarding typology are set out in *Psychological Types*, his second major work originally published in 1921 (Jung 1971). His theory of typology, especially the concept of introversion and extraversion, has been broadly incorporated into popular usage, and the widely utilized Myers–Briggs Type Indicator (MBTI) is based on Jung's typological theories.

Jung distinguishes between two basic attitudinal types, introverted and extraverted, which describe the individual's general orientation to the inner and outer worlds. According to Jung, the extravert has an outward movement of interest or libido toward the object and seeks communication and expression. The introvert has an inward movement of interest or libido away from the object toward the subject, i.e., the individual's own psychological processes.

These fundamental attitudinal orientations are experienced through a combination of four inter-related functions: thinking, feeling, sensation, and intuition. The thinking function is the capacity to order experience conceptually by analyzing, categorizing, and developing logical hierarchies. The feeling function does not refer to the capacity to experience affects, but rather is the capacity to develop a judgement of value, either good or bad. Typically, someone with a high degree of feeling function develops a strong sense of right and wrong and attunes to the moral or ethical implications of situations. The sensation function reflects capacity for attending to information, especially details, within one's environment that is gathered through sensory perception, e.g., hard data, visual images, movement, color, sounds, textures. Finally, the function of intuition reflects the capacity to see implications and possibility even when conclusive data is lacking. It is the ability to work with hunches and to receive and organize information on a subliminal level. Jung proposed that thinking and feeling stand in opposition to each other, i.e., that an individual may prefer thinking over feeling, or vice versa. Likewise, sensing and intuition are in opposition. Thinking and feeling refer to how an individual arrives at decisions, while sensation and intuition refer to how one gathers information. Jung summarizes the relationship between these functions as follows, "Sensation (i.e., sense perception) tells you that something exists; thinking tells you what it is; feeling tells you whether it is agreeable or not; and intuition tells you whence it comes and where it is going" (Jung 1964, p. 49). The way each of the functions is experienced and expressed will differ depending upon whether the individual is fundamentally extraverted or introverted in attitudinal orientation.

Synchronicity

Synchronicity is the term Jung coined to describe the meaningful but non-causal relationship between events, often describing the connection between intrapsychic experiences and outer-world events. For example, Jung (1952a) describes an encounter with a patient who dreamed of a scarab beetle. As she told Jung about it, a scarab-like beetle appeared at the window of his consulting room. Rather than dismissing the appearance of the beetle as a coincidence, Jung felt the appearance of the beetle reflected a meaningful correspondence between the patient's inner life and the world around the patient. Jung's concept of synchronicity grew out of discussions Jung had with Nobel prize-winning physicist Wolfgang Pauli on quantum field theory. Jung describes psyche and matter as being two inter-related manifestations of an underlying unified field:

> Since psyche and matter are contained in one and the same world, and moreover are in continuous contact with one another and ultimately rest on irrepresentable, transcendental factors, it is not only possible but fairly probable, even, that psyche and matter are two different aspects of one and the same thing. The synchronicity phenomena point … in this direction, for they show that the nonpsychic can behave like the psychic and vice versa, without there being any causal connection between them.
>
> (Jung 1954b, ¶418)

Notes

1 "Energy necessarily depends on a pre-existing polarity, without which there could be no energy" (Jung 1917, ¶115).
2 "Displacement of energy occurs only when there is a gradient, a difference in potential expressed psychologically by the pairs of opposites" (Jacobi 1973, p. 56).
3 "The shuttling to and from of arguments and affects represents the transcendent function of opposites. The confrontation of the two positions generates a tension charged with energy and creates a living third thing … a movement out of the suspension between opposites, a living birth that leads to a new level of being, a new situation. The

transcendent function manifests itself as a quality of conjoined opposites" (Jung 1958, ¶189).

4 "The psychological mechanism that transforms energy is the symbol" (Jung 1948c, ¶88).

5 "But if the individuation process is made conscious, consciousness must confront the unconscious and a balance between the opposites must be found. As this is not possible through logic, one is dependent on symbols which make the irrational union of opposites possible" (Jung 1952b, ¶755).

Suggestions for Further Reading

Classic Papers

Jung, C.G. (1948c). On psychic energy. In *CW8*. Princeton, NJ: Princeton University Press.

Jung, C.G. (1952a). Synchronicity: An acausal connecting principle. In *CW8*. Princeton, NJ: Princeton University Press.

Jung, C.G. (1958). The transcendent function. In *CW8*. Princeton, NJ: Princeton University Press.

Additional Recommended Reading

Harding, M.E. (1963). *Psychic Energy: Its Source and Its Transformation*. Princeton, NJ: Princeton University Press.

Stein, M. (1998). *Jung's Map of the Soul: An Introduction*. Chicago, IL: Open Court.

Chapter 7

Jungian Perspectives on Defenses and Psychopathology

Defenses

In analytical psychology, the study and analysis of defenses is relatively undeveloped, in part because Jung himself rarely wrote about defenses (Van Eenwyk 1991; Kalsched 2010, 2013). In many Jungian training programs, specific emphasis on understanding the function of defense mechanisms in the overall psychic system is often lacking and little guidance is offered in how to engage defenses effectively in the service of the patient's analysis. The Jungians who do emphasize the importance of defenses in analysis tend to borrow ideas from other schools of psychoanalytic thought, such as Melanie Klein, Heinz Kohut, Donald Winnicott, and Otto Kernberg (Van Eenwyk 1991). Kalsched describes the status of defenses in analytical psychology as such:

> I found only a few references to the word 'defense' in Jung's collected works, and all of them are to the higher-order repressive defenses. … Jung [insistently] pulls the idea of defense back into his compensation model, and how little he was aware of, or interested in, 'primitive' defenses and their destructive potential. … Following Jung, very few analytical psychologists think in terms of defense as such but rather in terms of one-sidedness and compensation by the unconscious. … Jungians have rarely recognized the ubiquity of defenses in psychological life, certainly not the pathological defenses we're talking about today.
>
> (2010, pp. 16–17)

DOI: 10.4324/9781003223511-8

Van Eenwyk points out that, "The lack of a specific theory of defences creates a certain discontinuity between Jung's and other psychoanalytic schools of thought" (1991, p. 142). Other psycho-analytic orientations typically divide the commonly recognized defenses into primary and secondary defenses (McWilliams 1994, pp. 96–144). Primary defenses, which are also referred to as primi-tive defenses, are seen as less developed and less adaptive. Primary defenses involve a blurring of the boundaries or separation between self and other. These defenses are typically utilized in early child-hood before stable ego functioning has been established but continue to be relied on into adulthood, especially in patients with trauma, psychosis, or personality disorders. Everyone maintains the capacity to fall into primitive, primary defenses because we all processed and managed our experiences via these processes during our pre-egoic infancy. Therefore, with personality and psychotic disorders, it is the relative absence of mature, secondary defenses that defines these conditions rather than the presence of primary defenses. The pri-mary defenses encountered include withdrawal, denial, omnipotent control, primitive idealization and devaluation, projection, introjec-tion, projective identification, splitting, and dissociation. Secondary defenses, which are also referred to as 'higher order defenses,' are generally seen as more developed coping strategies and are more associated with an alteration of one's interior world rather than the boundaries between self and other. Secondary defenses include repression, regression, isolation, intellectualization, rationalization, moralization, compartmentalization, undoing, turning against self, displacement, reaction formation, reversal, identification, acting out, sexualization, and sublimation.

The lack of emphasis on defenses in analytical psychology is somewhat paradoxical because Jung's model of the psyche is fun-damentally built around the process of dissociation. Jung specifi-cally indicates that the primary structures of the psyche, complexes, are created through dissociation in which complexes are "kept apart by strong emotional barriers" (1973a, ¶719). Jung's dissociative model of the psyche involves multiple autono-mous complexes, the ego, and the Self. Jung hypothesized that neurosis was a result of dissociation between these complexes. He referred to this as the dissociability of the psyche (1954b, ¶365) and viewed it as occurring in the healthy as well as the sick individual. Elsewhere, Jung highlights the process of dissociation in the transitory activation of various complexes and the temporary displacement of the ego as the center of consciousness:

> A certain *abaissement du niveau mental*, i.e., a weakness in the hierarchical order of the ego, is enough to set the instinctive urges and desires in motion and bring about a dissociation of personality – a multiplication of its centres of gravity.
>
> (1946, ¶361)

As mentioned earlier, in some way each autonomous complex is the result of a dissociation within the psyche and, as mentioned in Chapter 4, each complex has its own uniquely organized set of preferred defense mechanisms. In contemporary Jungian complex theory, all complexes have specific safety agendas and defensive strategies designed to carry out those safety agendas. When a complex is activated, it displaces the ego as the central organ of experience and temporarily becomes a stand-in or substitute ego, mobilizing its own unique set of defenses.

Defenses in Jung's Collected Works

As Kalsched (2010) mentions in his critique of Jung's treatment of defenses, Jung often speaks of defense processes in terms of their functioning as compensation for one-sidedness in the individual psyche. In his writing, Jung primarily refers to projection, introjection, repression, dissociation, regressive restoration of the persona, identification with the persona, and identification with a mana personality. The three later defenses can be considered Jung's unique contribution to the theory of defenses.

Regressive restoration of the persona refers to a defensive process utilized when an individual feels overwhelmed or threatened by the psychological risk associated with the development of the personality or life. It is seen when an individual approaches a new development or a new orientation in life but finds themselves confronted by obstacles or challenges – whether internal or external. In the face of adversity, the individual abandons their efforts and reverts to an earlier stage of persona development – for example a nurse who decides he wants to become a physician but finds the studies overwhelming and concludes they were happier being a nurse.

Identification with the persona refers to a defensive state of self-deception and deception of others in which there is little, if any, differentiation made between ego identity and persona. Persona is the adaptive presentation which is developed to present an acceptable personal image to the outer world. The persona typically is seen as standing in compensatory relationship to the shadow. When the persona is identified with, then greater pressure is placed on keeping the shadow repressed. To the extent that ego-consciousness is identified with the persona, the neglected inner life (personified in the shadow and anima or animus) is activated in compensation.

Identification with a mana personality is a concept Jung used to describe the inflationary effect of assimilating autonomous unconscious contents, particularly those associated with anima and animus which he saw as archetypally based: "The mana-personality is a dominant of the collective unconscious, the well-known archetype of the mighty man in the form of hero, chief, magician, medicine-man, saint, the ruler of men and spirits, the friend of God" (1966, ¶377). The defensive use of the unconscious identification with a mana personality is most likely in cases of severe depression, i.e., the inflationary experience of identifying with the mana personality would provide temporary relief from the depressive symptoms, in function not unlike Klein's (1935) concept of manic defenses against grief and depression.

Defenses of the Self

Another Jungian addition to the conceptualization of defenses was introduced by Michael Fordham (1974). Building on earlier work by Stein (1967), he introduced the term 'defenses of the Self' to describe the intense primary defenses mobilized by the patient to actively attack or nullify the analyst's efforts to make contact and facilitate change. He indicates that this takes place through silence, ritualization of the sessions, or explicit attacks on the analyst, the analytic frame, and the analytic method. He proposes that these defenses were not mobilized to protect the ego, nor are they reflective of a particular complex. Rather Fordham sees the mobilization of these defenses as an attempt to avoid the dismantling of a pseudo-maturity acquired early in life to compensate for failures in parenting or to avoid uncovering feelings of emptiness, formless terror, and dread. Fordham characterized defenses of the Self as the most virulent form of resistance. Wilfred Bion (1959) addressed similar clinical phenomena with his concept 'attacks on linking' which he described as "destructive attacks which the patient makes on anything which is felt to have the function of linking one object with another" (p. 308).

Kalsched (1996, 2013, 2015) has built upon the work of Bion and Fordham in proposing an archetypally based "self-care" system designed to protect the most regressed parts of traumatized individuals which he terms "the personal spirit." The primary activity of the self-care system is to keep these regressed parts "safe" by terrorizing them when any possibility of connection with other objects emerges. This creates an intensely hostile inner object world designed to ensure survival but without any hope of transformation or integration.

Elsewhere, Kalsched provides a fervent appeal for a fuller incorporation of defenses into Jungian psychoanalysis:

> To summarize, I suggest that we need to include the reality of primitive defenses in our Jungian metapsychology, and we need it for three reasons. First, it provides us with a better understanding of a certain species of violent aggression in the human psyche and this, in turn, gives us an inter- as well as an intra-psychic explanation for the origins of evil and human destructiveness. Second, it aligns our theory in a more productive way with recent findings in the fields of neuroscience and attachment theory. And finally, it helps us to intervene in a more relevant way with our patients
>
> (2010, p. 17).

Psychopathology

In general, Jung's conceptualization of psychopathology is primarily rooted in his ideas of the movement of psychic energy and an underlying interplay of opposites in psychological experience.

For Jung, psychopathology or maladaptation arises from rigidity or one-sidedness in the conscious attitude of the individual, "One could say that the function of the unconscious in mental disturbances is essentially a compensation of the conscious content" (Jung 1960, ¶465). Jung indicates that the function of the unconscious is to compensate for the one-sidedness of a rigid conscious position: "The principal function of the unconscious is to effect a compensation and to produce a balance. All extreme conscious tendencies are softened and toned down through a counter-impulse in the unconscious" (Jung 1960, ¶449). This perspective emphasizes the self-regulating aspects of the psyche: "The psyche is a self-regulating system that maintains its equilibrium just as the body does. Every process that goes too far immediately and inevitably calls forth compensations" (Jung 1931/1934, ¶330). While this perspective facilitates a focus on the patient's unconscious processes that contribute to healing, as Kalsched (2010) mentioned above, an overly exclusive focus on the compensatory, self-regulating aspects of the psyche can lead the analyst to overlook the more destructive aspects of the psyche.

Jung emphasized the treatment of the whole person rather than the treatment of a particular condition, e.g., "We can therefore never hope for a thorough cure from a treatment restricted to the illness itself, but only from a treatment of the personality as a whole" (Jung 1960/1969, ¶684), and "In therapy the problem is always the whole person, never the symptom alone. We must ask questions which challenge the whole personality" (Jung 1965, p. 117). As a result of this emphasis, Jung was dismissive of diagnosis in general:

> Psychogenic disturbances, quite unlike organic diseases, are atypical and individual. … Though we cannot do without such a nomenclature, we use it with the feeling that we have not said very much. As a rule, the diagnosis does not greatly matter since the needs and the difficulties of the treatment have to do with quite other factors than the more or less fortuitous diagnosis. And because there are only individual illnesses, they practically never follow a typical course on which a specific diagnosis could be based.
>
> (Jung 1954/1966, ¶540)

He also proposed that the content and function of the patient's complexes were more essential to the therapeutic process than their diagnosis (Chapter 4 contains a more in-depth treatment of the relationship between complexes, neuroses, and dissociation):

> Diagnosis is a highly irrelevant affair since, apart from affixing a more or less lucky label to a neurotic condition, nothing is gained by it, least of all as regards prognosis and therapy. … The diagnosis of any particular psychoneurosis means, at most, that some form of psychotherapy is indicated. … Whether a person is suffering from hysteria, or an anxiety neurosis, or a phobia, means little. … In psychotherapy the recognition of disease rests much less on the clinical picture than on the content of complexes.
>
> (Jung 1954/1966, ¶195–196)

While Jung did not place particular emphasis on diagnostic categories, several Jungian authors have addressed a variety of diagnostic categories and the broader issue of psychopathology, e.g., Kalsched (1996, 2013) and Wirtz (2020) address the issue of trauma, Schwartz-Salant (1982) and Jacoby (1990) examine narcissism, Schwartz-Salant (1989) also offers a Jungian exploration of borderline personality disorder, Cowan (1982) addresses masochism, Bisagni (2019) surveys obsessive compulsive disorder, and Samuels (1991) offers a wide-ranging collection of papers on psychopathology from a Jungian perspective.

Suggestions for Further Reading

Dougherty, N. and West, J. (2007). *The Matrix and Meaning of Character*. London: Routledge.

Fordham, M. (1974). *Defences of the Self*. J. Anal. Psychol., *19* (2): 192–199.

Kalsched, D. (2015). Revisioning Fordham's "Defences of the Self" in light of modern relational theory and contemporary neuroscience. J. Anal. Psychol., *60*: 477–496.

Samuels, A. (Ed.) (1991). *Psychopathology: Contemporary Jungian Perspectives*. New York: Guilford.

Van Eenwyk, J. (1991). The analysis of defences. *J. Anal. Psychol.*, *36*: 141–163.

Chapter 8

Technique in Jungian Psychoanalysis

Analytic technique refers to the methods or processes by which an analytic interaction takes place. That is, how the analyst listens, begins and ends an analysis, establishes the analytic frame,[1] develops a therapeutic working alliance,[2] works within the transference–countertransference matrix, engages the patient's defenses and resistance, works with dreams, and interprets the analytic interaction. Technique addresses the process of analytic work rather than the content that emerges during the work.

Freud laid out the fundamental principles of technique in psychoanalysis in a series of ten papers published between 1910 and 1919 (Freud 1959). While these guidelines have been re-examined and modified (e.g., Fenichel 1941; Greenson 1967; Etchegoyen 2005), Freud's fundamental guidelines on technique continue to be utilized in contemporary psychoanalysis even though many of Freud's theories regarding the nature of unconscious processes and development of the personality have been modified or discarded (Rubovits-Seitz 2002).

Historically, Jungians have held a more ambivalent attitude about guidelines regarding technique in general and interpretation in particular (Zinkin 1969; Charlton 1986). As Dieckmann (1991) points out, Jungians generally have an aversion to addressing technical guidelines for undertaking an analysis with the exception of dream interpretation and active imagination. Numerous volumes have been written detailing guidelines for Jungian dream interpretation and active imagination, yet there are only a few books which address the general fundamentals of technique from a Jungian perspective. As Bovensiepen (2002) puts it:

DOI: 10.4324/9781003223511-9

Even today, several of my Jungian colleagues and I frequently experience a certain gap between Jung's topical theoretical conceptions of the unconscious and transformability of the psyche and his lack of theory for analytic technique. ... Or perhaps, to express it more poetically, Jungians like ourselves too often have our heads in the clouds, and we can learn from psychoanalytical treatment technique to bring us back down to earth.

(p. 242)

Historically, the primary exception to the Jungian ambivalence toward the technical aspects of analysis has been Michael Fordham and the Society of Analytical Psychology in London (Astor 1995; Samuels 1985). Fordham and other analysts of the SAP began incorporating elements of psychoanalytic technique in areas where they felt there was inadequate development of the Jungian model. This hybrid approach came to be referred to as the developmental approach.

Apart from the developmental perspective, Jungian analytic training often tends to underemphasize technique. As a result, important tools for working analytically are not well developed. While most general introductions to Jungian theory and practice contain a chapter or two on technique, in the Jungian literature published in English there are only a handful of texts focusing primarily on the technique of analysis from a Jungian perspective, primarily Dieckmann (1991), Fordham (1978), and Fordham et al. (1978). In comparison, there are hundreds of volumes on dreams and hundreds of volumes exploring various archetypal themes.

In my experience, as a teacher and supervisor, many Jungian analytic candidates feel rather uncertain about how to proceed in the analytic situation when not involved with dream interpretation or active imagination. They often have difficulty recognizing and engaging the patient's emerging unconscious material when the symbolism is not readily identified as such within the analytic context.

The general avoidance of technique within the Jungian world can largely be traced back to Jung's attitude towards technique which carried on in the generations that followed him. Adler summarizes the traditional Jungian position as follows:

> One of the main differences between Analytical Psychology and other schools lies in the undogmatic approach of Analytical Psychology to each individual case. The basic presupposition from which Analytical Psychology starts is that each patient has his own particular and 'personal' psychology necessitating an approach which varies with each individual case. ... Such a conception must obviously involve a considerable limitation on general technique, since the whole point of a technique is to provide certain universally applicable rules.
>
> (1967, p. 23)

Typologically, Jung was an intuitive (like many who have been drawn to his ideas) who had an aversion to methodological approaches. Dehing (1992, p. 42) indicates that Jung detested any sort of systemization. Jung also established his position as a reaction against elements of Freud's theory and technique (Zinkin 1969). Additionally, Jung felt that the pursuit of analytical psychology was so unique to the individual personality of the practitioner that he did not believe one should provide specific guidelines as to the practice of analytical psychology. While Jung's adoption of an anti-methodological position may have been useful in differentiating analytical psychology from Freudian psychoanalysis, I propose that he also discarded an important element of the transformative process.

According to Fordham, the lack of focus on technique had a detrimental effect on the development of well-rounded analysts: "The methods used by Jung, and more so by his followers, were not applicable often in the rough and tumble of everyday psychotherapy when the careful analysis of sexuality and childhood was often needed but neglected" (1998, pp. 56–57). Fordham is alluding to the reality that many patients presenting for therapy or analysis are not initially well-suited for a classical Jungian or archetypally focused analysis. Such a situation arises with patients who arrive for therapy not yet functioning at a symbolic level and

still needing to address areas of immature psychological development, deficits in identity and self-structure, or experiencing difficulty with affective-behavioral regulation.

Kirsch (2000) captures the essence of these two primary attitudes towards technique in analytical psychology:

> Jung eschewed the word 'technique,' but there was a general
> way in which he worked. He used dream analysis, active
> imagination, and amplification in face-to-face, relatively infre-
> quent sessions, and fostered an active dialectic between himself
> and his patient. Today there is wide variation in the use of these
> basic analytic methods. The more developmentally oriented Jun-
> gians use a couch, require more frequent sessions, interpret the
> transference, and focus less on dreams, amplification and active
> imagination.
>
> (2000, p. 247)

Zinkin argues that "both models are essential and complementary"
(1969, p. 131). I maintain that the divide between these two positions
can be diminished further and that a greater emphasis on technique
can be assimilated by analytical psychology without losing the analytic values so central to Jung's original model.

The Analytic Frame

In general, the concept of the analytic frame includes the physical
setup of the consulting room; the use of couch or chair; whether
to encourage the patient's use of free association; the frequency,
time, and duration of sessions; establishment of fees, including the
method and time of payment, use of insurance, or third-party
payment; handling of changes to the schedule, missed appoint-
ments, and vacations; guidelines for contact between sessions; the
issue of physical contact; and contact with outside parties. The
analytic frame is often misunderstood as a set of rules that define
analysis, rather than being understood as a set of parameters
which facilitate the emergence of unconscious material, and which
create a lens that facilitates understanding of what is happening in
the analytic encounter.

In the Jungian community, the analytic frame is often discussed through the alchemical metaphor favored by Jung, utilizing terms from alchemy, such as *vas hermeticum* (i.e., the hermetic vessel – a reference to the vase in which many alchemical operations were occurring – such as dissolving into solution, heating, distillation), or the *vas bene clausum* (i.e., the well-sealed vessel which does not allow contaminating elements to disrupt or distort the alchemical process occurring inside the vessel). In other words, the Jungian community often emphasizes the symbolic and ritual elements of the analytic frame.

In general, the average frequency of sessions in Jungian psychoanalysis is once per week. Those operating from the classical perspective offer several reasons for this. In Jungian psychoanalysis there is an emphasis on developing a dialectic process, between patient and analyst, but also between conscious and unconscious, which is also conceptualized as a dialectic process between ego and Self. This conceptualization is captured in Neumann's (1966) concept of the ego–Self axis. The ego–Self axis is a spatial metaphor which represents the degree of openness and interaction between the ego, i.e., the center of waking consciousness and identity, and the Self, i.e., the unconscious center of the personality as a whole and the central organizing principle of the psyche. One aim of the classical Jungian perspective is to facilitate the development of the ego–Self dialectic. From the classical perspective, when meeting weekly, the longer gap between sessions leaves more room for this ego–Self dialectic to emerge and reduces the patient's possibility of the patient becoming overly dependent on the analyst which might interfere with the development of the ego–Self dialectic. However, those who practice from the developmental perspective are much more likely to see patients two to four times a week. Those practicing from the developmental perspective place greater emphasis on the analysis of the transference–countertransference matrix, the importance of therapeutic regression, the use of analytic reverie, and the analysis of defenses; processes which become more readily available and more effectively engaged as frequency increases.

Similarly, distinctions also emerge in analytical psychology around the use of the analytic couch or the chair. Those practicing from a developmental perspective are much more likely to utilize the couch, feeling that it facilitates reflection, shared reverie, therapeutic regression, and greater focus on internal processes and states with an accompanying reduction in attention to social cues between analyst and patient, and greater freedom of associations. Those practicing from the classical and archetypal perspectives are much less likely to utilize the analytic couch, feeling that the face-to-face interaction allows a greater sense of equality between the analytic participants and discourages analytic regression.

Jungians often harbor a bias against the use of free association in the analytic process, especially by those practicing from the classical perspective. This bias stems from Jung's differentiation of his dream approach from Freud's. He felt Freud's encouraging his patients to free associate to their dream imagery often led the patient and analyst away from identifying and focusing on the primary complex reflected in the dream. In place of free association, Jung developed the use of 'directed association' in which the patient is brought back to the specific dream image repeatedly until the patient no longer produces associations to the image. In other words, in Freud's method of free association, if a patient dreamt of a dog, the patient would be asked, "what does a dog make you think of?" If the patient said, "it makes me think of the dog I had as a child," then they would be asked, "and what does the dog you had as a child bring to mind?" Instead, Jung would bring the patient back to the original dog in the dream and ask, "and what else does this dog make you think of?"

However, Jung's position against free association in terms of dreamwork has been carried over to all analytic interactions. The value of encouraging the patient to say whatever comes into their awareness during a session (i.e., free association) has been under-appreciated, although free association during analytic sessions is more common among developmental Jungians. Personally, I find that encouraging the use of free association during sessions encourages greater use of reverie, affords greater access to the imagination of the patient, and facilitates disclosure of thoughts and feelings that would typically be defended against.

Frequency of sessions, use of the analytic couch or chair, and the question of whether to encourage free association are the primary ways Jungian psychoanalysts are likely to differ from analysts of other psychoanalytic orientations. Apart from these three areas, Jungian psychoanalysts typically incorporate other elements of the analytic frame in a similar way as psychoanalysts from other perspectives.

Active Imagination

In addition to recommending directed association, it could also be argued that Jung replaced Freud's free association method with active imagination, a technique developed by Jung to facilitate the engagement and assimilation of unconscious processes (Jung 1958). In active imagination, the patient is encouraged to adopt a relaxed state and to concentrate on a specific figure, mood, or event and allow a chain of associative fantasies to emerge around the central theme selected. Active imagination has been described as "dreaming with open eyes" (Sharp 1991, p. 13). Jung engaged in extensive use of active imagination during his period of internal crisis following his split with Freud, the results of which are documented in *The Red Book* (2009) and *The Black Books* (2020).

Often the initial focus for an active imagination is selected from a recent dream, especially if the dream did not reach a resolution or was interrupted. Engaging in an active imagination around an unresolved dream is seen as an opportunity to dream the dream forward so that the resolution is revealed through waking fantasy. In active imagination, a relationship or stance is established with the internal flow of imagery, affects, and actions, yet the patient is encouraged to only attempt to influence the stance or actions of their own image (i.e., the dream ego) during active imagination and to let all other figures and events unfold autonomously, while in a relaxed but waking state. Jung proposed that the images appearing during an ongoing series of active imaginations take on a life of their own and unfold along their own internal logic. However, as I have argued (Winborn 2023), the patient's symbolic capacity should be taken into consideration, and active imagination should not be introduced with patients who do not have well-established symbolic capacity, i.e., who function at the concrete level of experience.

Jung saw active imagination as an activity primarily engaged in by the analysand, but initially facilitated by the analyst. It does not appear that Jung saw active imagination as something that was engaged in with another person as reverie is typically conceptualized (i.e., a bipersonal or intersubjective process). Active imagination is typically introduced during sessions, but the patient is also often encouraged to engage in active imagination outside of analytic sessions. Additionally, Jung also saw active imagination as a process introduced as an analysis was entering the later stages. He conceived of it as a useful process for the patient in terms of continuing an ongoing dialectic between ego consciousness and the unconscious after analysis concluded. Jungian analysts associated with the classical orientation are the most likely to utilize active imagination with their patients. Hannah (1981) offers one of the most comprehensive reviews of the concept and method of active imagination, including detailed case examples. Recognizing that not all patients are equally prepared to engage in active imagination and that some patients find the prospect of active imagination unfamiliar or intimidating, Kast (1993) has developed a useful series of progressive exercises for cultivating the patient's capacity for engaging in imaginal processes.

Davidson (1966) extends Jung's concept of active imagination by proposing that all of analysis, in particular the patient's transference, is a "form of lived-through active imagination" (p. 143). Schaverien (2007), building on Davidson's position, suggests that the analyst can utilize active imagination to deepen understanding of countertransference responses, and proposes that active imagination can be thought of as nearly synonymous with reverie.

Transference–Countertransference Matrix

Jung's writing contains mixed positions on transference and countertransference. Jung recalls an encounter with Freud in 1907, during their active relationship:

> Suddenly he [Freud] asked me out of the blue, "And what do you think about the transference?" I replied with the deepest conviction that it was the alpha and omega of the analytical

method, whereupon he said, "Then you have grasped the main thing."

(1954/1966, ¶358)

However, Jung goes on to state, "The great importance of the transference has often led to the mistaken idea that it is absolutely indispensable for a cure. ... I personally am always glad when there is only a mild transference or when it is practically unnoticeable" (1954/1966, ¶359). While ambivalent from a subjective perspective, Jung also recognizes the fundamental nature of the transference–countertransference matrix for the analytic process, seeing transference as an avenue for understanding the patient, and acknowledging the reciprocal influence between patient and analyst:

The transference phenomenon is an inevitable feature of every thorough analysis, for it is imperative that the doctor should get into the closest possible touch with the patient's line of psychological development. One could say that in the same measure as the doctor assimilates the intimate psychic contents of the patient into himself, he is in turn assimilated as a figure into the patient's psyche.

(1954/1966, ¶283)

Additionally, while still in relationship with Freud, it was Jung who insisted that every potential analyst should undergo analysis themselves (i.e., a training analysis) to reduce the likelihood that the analyst's own complexes and unresolved conflicts would distort the analyst's understanding and effective utilization of their countertransference to the patient (Samuels, Shorter, and Plaut 1986).

Jung's saw the transference as taking place primarily through the process of projection (Jung 1935, ¶312). He concluded transferences could be understood both 'reductively,' i.e., originating in the patient's historical experiences, or 'synthetically,' i.e., that the transference also reflects experiences of the patient necessary for continued development. In this respect, Jung's concept of a synthetic element in analysis parallels closely Kohut's concept of the selfobject (1977), which does not refer directly to an internal or external object, but rather the function which that figure serves in terms of the structuring and cohesion of the self. In other words, both Jung and Kohut were interested in not only what patterns from the past were being repeated in the transference but also the ways the transference provided needed experiences to facilitate the development of the individual and to fill in deficits in the self-structure that reflect earlier disruptions with primary caregivers.

Jung also proposed that transferences were not entirely personal in nature, i.e., that the patient's transference to the analyst often included archetypal patterns being projected onto the analyst (Jung 1917, ¶163). In fact, Jung's longest treatise on the transference–countertransference matrix, *The Psychology of the Transference* (1946), is based on an alchemical text first published in 1550, the *Rosarium philosophorum*. Jung interprets the images associated with the text, which depict various stages of transformation and interaction, from a psychological and spiritual perspective. Jung felt that the images portrayed in this alchemical text paralleled and informed the processes he encountered in his sessions with analysands. Jung's utilization of alchemy as his primary device for describing theses phenomena may make it difficult for those unfamiliar with his writing to grasp the essence of the underlying themes, but in this work his concepts of the 'subtle body,' the 'psychoid realm,' and '*coniunctio*' parallel concepts found in contemporary psychoanalysis, such as the 'analytic third' and the 'intersubjective field.'

Jung focuses on the first ten woodcuts from a series of twenty images. The woodcuts and the accompanying text depict an incestuous love story between a king and queen. The images portray an alchemical fountain or bath which serves as the *vas hermeticum* to contain the various energies activated in their interactions. The two figures move through various alchemical stages as the woodcuts progress, dissolving and separation (*separatio* and *divisio*), joining of opposites (*coniunctio*), blackening or darkening (*nigredo*), purification (*mundificatio*), and whitening or transformation (*albedo*). Jung utilized alchemy as a metaphor for a variety of psychological processes, including the transference and countertransference matrix. Samuels indicates that Jung's use of the alchemical metaphor helps us bear in mind that "the inter-personal and the imaginal are equal partners and the technical implication is that content analysis and process analysis can, must coexist" (1989, p. 177).

In terms of post-Jungian developments with the transference–countertransference matrix, both Sedgwick (1994) and Wiener (2009) provide comprehensive overviews of the Jungian con-ceptualization of transference–countertransference in analysis, as well as case illustrations and recommendations for working with the transference–countertransference phenomenon. Sedgwick (1994) also reviews the Jungian model of transference–countertransference refer-red to as the "wounded healer" model (Guggenbühl-Craig 1971; Groesbeck 1975). Like the alchemical model depicted in Jung's *The Psychology of the Transference*, the wounded healer model is also based on an archetypally based metaphor, i.e., the motif of the healer who heals the patient through the healer's own woundedness. This symbolic theme emerges primarily from the myth of Asclepius and Chiron in Greek mythology. Briefly, Asclepius is the offspring of a liaison between the Greek god Apollo and Coronis, a Thessalian princess. While there are several variations of the myth, Asclepius is ultimately taken from or abandoned by Cor-onis and is raised by the centaur Chiron who teaches Asclepius the healing arts. Chiron himself was the wounded and abandoned offspring of Cronos and Rhea who was raised by Apollo and instructed in the ways of healing. Asclepius becomes a heroic healing figure to the Greeks and is often depicted with a snake-entwined staff (which is passed into contemporary time in the image of the medical caduceus – the rod with two entwined snakes capped by the wings of Hermes). After his death, at the request of Apollo, Zeus resurrects Asclepius as a god and gives him a place on Olympus.

Cwik (2011, 2017), drawing upon Jung's concept of active ima-gination, Ogden's concept of the analytic third (2004), and Bion's concept of reverie (1962/1983), proposes an intersubjective process he refers to as "associative dreaming." While Cwik conceptualizes associative dreaming as a reciprocally constellated analytic third which has implications for the analyst's countertransference, he also indicates that the focus of his concept extends beyond the transference–countertransference matrix alone, indicating that emergent images, sensations, and memories also reflect "micro-activations of the transcendent function" (Cwik 2011, p. 14). Using the illustration of a myth entering the analyst's mind during an analytic session, his focus is on an intuitive internal exploration of wondering how and why that particular myth entered the analyst's mind and what the myth says about the analytic field constellated between analyst and patient. Cwik goes on to describe how the analyst's "associative dreaming" might then be introduced into the analytic exchange either implicitly or explicitly. Samuels (1989) describes a similar process but utilizes the metaphor of the *mundus imaginalis* (i.e, imaginal world), the analyst's embodied experience, and countertransference constellations. Samuels describes the *mundus imaginalis* as a shared dimension of experience, similar to Winnicott's concept of 'transitional space' (Winnicott 1971) and Cwik's concept of associative dreaming. For Samuels, this shared experience is fundamentally an embodied experience which "can be placed firmly *within* the imaginal real without *forgetting* that there are two people present" (1989, p. 173, italics in original).

Interpretation

As mentioned earlier, the subject of technique or method receives significantly less emphasis in most Jungian psychoanalytic training programs than it does in many other schools of psychoanalytic training. This tendency is particularly pronounced in the area of analytic interpretation. As of this writing, there is only one text which exclusively addresses the technique of analytic interpretation from a Jungian perspective (Winborn 2019).

The origins of psychoanalytic interpretation can be traced back to a twelfth-century Latin term, *interpretati*, which means to explain, expound, or understand (Blue and Harrang 2016). Interpretation is also connected to the field of hermeneutics, "the study of the methodological principles of interpretation" (Merriam-Webster n.d.), often in reference to the textual analysis of literature, scripture, and alchemy as well as art and history. In analytic therapy, at the most fundamental level,

"Interpretation seeks to make conscious the unconscious" (Etchegoyen 2005, p. 386).

Contrary to some perceptions, a psychoanalytic interpretation is not everything that is spoken to the patient in a session. It is a specific type of verbal interaction which sets it apart from other types of therapeutic utterances – such as asking questions, reframing patient statements, affective mirroring, empathic statements, or reassurance. As Oremland (1991) points out, while all these interventions may contribute to the progress of an analysis, only interpretation is specifically intended to facilitate the engagement and understanding of the patient's unconscious.

In *Interpretation in Jungian Analysis* (Winborn 2019), I provide an overview of the theory of analytic interpretation from various psychoanalytic approaches and from the Jungian perspective, as well as examining the issue of technique in the Jungian community, the integration of Jungian theory and archetypal metaphors in the crafting of an interpretation, and a review of the relevant research on interpretation. Additionally, I emphasize the importance of directing interpretations towards the activated complex(es) of the patient rather than organizing the interpretation around the conscious ego concerns of patient. I refer to this interpretive shift as 'speaking with the complex' versus speaking about the complex.

Only a handful of other Jungian authors have articulated a theory or method for interpretation. Fordham (1978, 1979, 1991a) was instrumental in incorporating aspects of psychoanalytic technique, in particular interpretation, into the field of analytical psychology. Much of Fordham's material on interpretation parallels the model developed by psychoanalytic practitioners. Fordham elaborates on the use of interpretation in the analysis of primitive mental states, articulates a model of interpretation that shifts the focus from the reductive-synthetic comparison to a model emphasizing the differentiation of self and not-self experiences, and describes the modifications of the interpretative method when encountering defenses of the Self.

Quite illuminating and thought-provoking is a debate that occurred in print between Fordham (1991a, 1991b) and Schwartz-Salant (1991) regarding the nature of interpretation, the effectiveness of interpretation in the engagement of primitive mental states, the analyst's use of their own experience in formulating interpretations, and the impact of the 'analytic third' on the process of interpretation. Their debate serves as a useful introduction to the concept of interpretation and the diverse possibilities or positions inherent in the interpretative process as well as providing the readers an opportunity for vicarious evaluation of their own perspective on interpretation.

In addition to the positions articulated in the Fordham and Schwartz-Salant debate, Dieckmann (1991) provides a useful introductory chapter on interpretation. His articulation of the relationship between interpretation and the working through of the patient's complexes is particularly useful, as is his focus on the importance of reductive interpretation for the integration of the personal shadow. The central role of metaphor in Jungian analysis and interpretation is developed effectively by Siegelman (1990). Covington (1995) provides an articulate examination of the relationship between interpretation, the construction of the patient's personal narrative, and the development of the patient's identity.

Ledermann (1995) surveys the potential pitfalls of interpretation. She highlights the potential contra-indications for interpretation with patients with weak ego structure, the danger of premature interpretation, and the impact of the analyst's countertransference on the interpretive process. Like Ledermann, von der Tann (1999) provides a cautionary examination of interpretation. Rather than falling into the myth that there is one correct interpretation for each analytic moment, von der Tann emphasizes the multiplicity of possible interpretations, each of which may articulate some essential facet of the various psychological dimensions present in every analytic moment. He proposes that "every interpretation is influenced by countertransference, however unconscious or unidentified this might be" (1999, p. 62). Instead of searching for the mythical 'correct' interpretation he invokes Winnicott's concept of the 'good enough' experience as applied to the process of interpretation.

More recently Astor (2011) and Bisagni (2013) have continued the exploration of interpretation in analytical psychology. Astor

(2011) focuses on the language used for interpretation, how inter-pretations are delivered, the affective component of interpretations, and conceptualizing the level of experience the interpretation is focused on. He also emphasizes the importance of the listening process during the interpretive process, i.e., during the formulation, articulation, and reception phases of interpretation. Astor proposes that the use of language in interpretation potentially becomes more nuanced when Bion's (1970/1983) concepts of alpha function, dream thoughts, beta elements, and alpha elements are paired with Jung's concept of the transcendent function. Bisagni (2013) reviews the interaction between mental representation, empathy, somatic experience, and the language of interpretation. More specifically, he examines word choice as an expression of intentionality and action in the analytic setting. Bisagni also reviews some of the potential hypotheses regarding interpretation that emerge from findings in contemporary neuroscience.

Additional methods or techniques unique to Jungian psycho-analysis will be addressed in Chapter 9.

Notes

1 The analytic frame refers to general guidelines which shape how the analytic interaction will unfold.
2 Also referred to as the working relationship or analytic alliance. The therapeutic alliance refers to the capacity of the analytic couple to develop a sufficient level of mutual trust, intimacy, and curiosity for analytic work to proceed.

Suggestions for Further Reading

Technique in Jungian Analysis

Dieckmann, H. (1991). *Methods in Analytical Psychology: An Introduction*. Wilmette, IL: Chiron.

The Analytic Relationship and Frame

Braun, C. (2020). *The Therapeutic Relationship in Analytical Psychology: Theory and Practice*. London: Routledge.

The Transference–Countertransference Matrix

Wiener, J. (2009). *The Therapeutic Relationship: Transference, Counter-transference, and the Making of Meaning*. College Station, TX: Texas A&M University Press.

Interpretation

Winborn, M. (2019). *Interpretation in Jungian Analysis: Art and Technique*. London: Routledge.

Chapter 9

An Overview of Jungian Psychoanalytic Training

Currently, the International Association for Analytical Psychology (IAAP) is the only international organization overseeing training for Jungian psychoanalysts. All institutes and societies desiring to provide training in analytical psychology must apply for recognition by the IAAP and meet minimum standards in terms of having adequate faculty and organizational structure. However, each training group maintains autonomy in terms of curriculum planning, training requirements, and training model. The IAAP maintains minimum standards for Jungian psychoanalytic candidates in terms of requirements for hours of personal analysis, hours of supervision, hours of case colloquia, hours of didactic instruction, and number of patient hours, although many Jungian training groups require more hours than the minimum established by the IAAP. Jungian training groups evaluate their candidates in a variety of ways, i.e., through oral and written examinations on fundamental areas of knowledge, case reports, oral case presentations, papers on theoretical or archetypal themes, supervisor evaluations, or a formal thesis, although not all institutes employ all the evaluation methods listed.

While some Jungian training groups have a standard curriculum that each candidate cohort progresses through, the majority of training groups tend to have more variability in their curriculum depending upon which faculty are available during a given training cycle. Rather than having a standard curriculum, many Jungian institutes organize their training focus around a set of content areas which each graduating analyst is expected to have familiarity with as

DOI: 10.4324/9781003223511-10

well as competency. In the Inter-Regional Society of Jungian Analysts these content areas are organized as follows:

1   Theoretical Foundations (basic principles of analytical psychology, structure and function of the psyche, psychological types and functions, theory of dream interpretation, individuation process, complex theory, the association experiment, history of analytical psychology, comparative study of current psychoanalytic theories, comparative study of newer therapies, psychopathology, developmental psychology).
2   Archetypal Material (dreams and fantasies, mythology and folklore, interpretation of fairy tales, comparative religions, symbolic formulations, alchemy).
3   Fields Related to Analytical Psychology (anthropology – study of traditional cultures, social psychology, group dynamics, creativity in the arts).
4   The Practice of Jungian Analysis (practical use of dream interpretation, active imagination and other creative techniques, transference and countertransference, case seminars).

As the content areas illustrate, a significant portion of the recommended content areas focuses on dreams and on acquiring familiarity with a wide variety of archetypal themes through the study of mythology, fairy tales, religions, alchemy, and anthropology. In the Jungian curricula I am familiar with, I would estimate courses in these areas account for approximately 65–70 percent of the seminars being offered by many Jungian training groups. While this weighting leads to a very rich exposure to a wide range of metaphorical material, it can also leave other areas of theory and technique less developed. In other words, many Jungian training groups place much greater emphasis on the archetypal and symbolic content of emerging unconscious material and less emphasis on the process of analysis. In my experience,[1] psychoanalytic institutes devote significantly more of their curriculum to the development of the technical aspects of psychoanalysis (e.g., developing the analytic relationship, establishing the analytic frame, working with the transference–countertransference field, making effective interpretations, and analyzing defenses and resistance) and have significantly less emphasis on developing familiarity with metaphorical material than Jungians would. Of course, without a theory of archetypes, there would be little reason for an institute from another psychoanalytic perspective to offer such coursework.

The organization of psychoanalytic training around psycho-analytic core competencies is one of the significant developments in analytic training over the past 20 years (Barsness 2018). Most succinctly, the organization of training around core psychoanalytic competencies shifts the emphasis in the curriculum from what a candidate should be taught to what the candidate should be able to do in an analytic process with what they are taught (Tuckett 2005). However, the concept of core competency areas in Jungian analytic training has been slow to develop. In the Jungian literature, there has only been one article addressing the value of incorporating core competencies into the organization of Jungian analytic training (Wiener 2007). However, recently there has been a book published on core competencies in Jungian psychoanalysis, emerging from a working group of the IAAP (Gudaitė and Kelly 2022).

In addition, to the training in active imagination, dreams, and working with transference and countertransference commonly found in most Jungian training programs, many Jungian candi-dates take elective training in an expressive therapy modality, such as the expressive arts (usually focused on painting, drawing, crea-tive writing, or drama therapy) (e.g., Swan-Foster 2017), music therapy (Kroeker 2019), or movement and dance (Chodorow 1991). Training in sandplay therapy is taken up during training by many Jungian candidates during their training, often undergoing an extensive certification process through one of the organizing bodies of sandplay therapy. Sandplay therapy is a nonverbal, therapeutic intervention that makes use of a sandbox, toy and miniature figures, small objects, and sometimes water, to create scenes of miniature worlds that reflect a person's unconscious processes (Weinrib 2004). All these modalities are more likely to be incorporated by candidates and analysts practicing from a classical orientation within analytical psychology. In general, each of these modalities can be thought of as serving a similar function as free association, i.e., facilitating the expression of unconscious processes.

Because of the emphasis on archetypal themes and the concept of synchronicity, some institutes also offer electives in astrology, I-Ching, or tarot (e.g., Greene 2018). This might seem odd or surprising to someone not familiar with analytical psychology. Each of these methods of 'divination' is seen as being fundamentally based upon archetypal patterns. When utilized, rather than being used to 'forecast the future,' these modalities are incorporated in terms of a 'reading.' The pattern which emerges during the reading is discussed in terms of the patient's associations to the material. There is an underlying assumption that a synchronicity between the patient and the archetypal patterns portrayed in the materials is potentially activated through the process, increasing the likelihood that a pattern meaningful to the patient's psychological situation will emerge.

Note

1 From 2013–2022, I served on the American Board for Accreditation in Psychoanalysis (ABAP), including six years as the Chair for the Committee on Accreditation, which accredited psychoanalytic institutes in the United States from a wide variety of theoretical orientations, including three Jungian institutes. In addition, I have served on the Training Committee of the IRSJA and as a seminar coordinator for the Memphis-Atlanta Jungian Seminar (a local training seminar of the IRSJA).

Suggestions for Further Reading

Jung, C.G. and Kerenyi, C. (1949). *Essays on a Science of Mythology.* New York: Harper.

Kast, V. (1996) The clinical use of fairy tales by a 'classical' Jungian analyst. *Psychoanal. Rev.*, *83*: 509–523.

Shearer, A. (2004). On the making of myths: Mythology in training. *J. of Jungian Theory and Practice, 6 (2)*: 1–14.

Chapter 10

Reflections from My Practice as a Jungian Psychoanalyst

My work as an analyst revolves around the developmental perspective in analytical psychology. I have also been deeply influenced by the work of Wilfred Bion and consider my orientation to be a hybrid of the Jungian and Bionian models. Looking back over my involvement with analytical psychology and psychoanalysis, I am content with how things have evolved.

I was initially drawn to analytical psychology by Jung's focus on dreams, the dialectic between consciousness and the unconscious, and the spiritual dimension of life. I did not experience the same attraction to the rather dry version of Freud I was exposed to as an undergraduate major in psychology. It was only during my later studies in analytical psychology, that I came to appreciate the perspectives offered by Freud, Klein, Winnicott, Bion, Searles, Fairbairn, Kohut, Ogden, Ferro, Civitarese, and many others. The focus on technique, interpretation, and early life experience found in psychoanalysis is now well ingrained in my clinical work. I find the field of comparative psychoanalysis extremely stimulating, but the greater value of such study lies in how an understanding of various models of psychoanalytic thought broadens and enriches my clinical practice.

While I am comfortable and satisfied with my choice to become a Jungian, I am always foremost a psychoanalyst. Although I may refer to myself as Jungian psychoanalyst, it is an acknowledgement that my Jungian orientation contributes in significant ways to the way I practice psychoanalysis. My ongoing journey is not guided by an allegiance to particular figure or theoretical

DOI: 10.4324/9781003223511-11

system. Rather I am guided by an ongoing process of assembling an amalgam of analytic approaches which complement and compensate each other, filling in the gaps found in any theory or technique, i.e., taking the 'best' elements of Jungian psychoanalysis and combining those with the useful elements of the other psychoanalytic approaches.

I share Wallerstein's (1988, 1992) position that what unites all psychoanalytic orientations is not differences but a specific commonality, that we all are engaged in the experience of the unconscious as it manifests in the consulting room, no matter how different our theoretical metaphors for discussing and describing that experience: "My thesis is that what unites us is our shared focus on the clinical interactions in our consulting rooms, the phenomena encompassed by the 'present unconscious'" (1988, p. 20). Although I don't expect this to happen, in my mind, an ideal situation is one in which there wouldn't be a need to designate which theoretical orientation we are affiliated with – that it would all be a focus on the process of analysis. After all, all models of psychoanalysis share a fundamental aim of engaging with unconscious processes, despite theoretical differences in how the unconscious is understood. It seems likely that our identification with historical figures and movements in the psychoanalytic field will always be present to some degree. It also seems likely that many will not feel comfortable with a poly-theoretical psychoanalytic perspective, however, I suspect there are few analysts practicing exclusively from one theoretical perspective. Also, I imagine those entering the analytic profession will always need a fundamental training in one orientation or system and that over time they will add other elements to that foundation.

In retrospect, I might have found my way into the psychoanalytic world through many different orientations, but there are elements of analytical psychology I would not want to relinquish. The emphasis on spiritual experience and the broad cultural and anthropological perspectives brought in through archetypal themes in analytical psychology also remain significant to me. Additionally, Jung's emphasis on creativity, imagination, the discovery of meaning, and the prospective nature of the psyche all remain essential for me.

While the universals of human experience expressed through Jung's archetypal theory were captivating for me in my early involvement with analytical psychology, over the years I've become more focused on the specificity and uniqueness of the individual and the narrative they are living out, as well as the uniqueness of each analytic dyad, i.e., "each interaction between persons is unique, unpredictable, and specific to them and that moment" (Bacal 2011, p. ix). I believe one of the most important skills of the analyst is the capacity for pattern recognition and the ability to communicate those patterns to the patient in a digestible way. In many respects, analysis is the construction of the narrative the patient is living out (Covington 1995), but it should also serve to familiarize the patient with how their psyche functions. In session, my focus is often on the smaller elements of transformational change, such as the patient's ability to experience and assimilate their affects, increases in reflective functioning and symbolic capacity, the creation of moments of meaning, and increases in self-agency.

I do utilize archetypal and cultural amplifications routinely in my practice, engage in dream work, and frequently utilize complex theory in reflecting on my patients. However, I utilize Jung's concept of archetypes as a way of speaking about universal elements of human experiences rather than as innate encoded patterns waiting to be activated. From a theoretical perspective, it is important to assess Jung's theory of archetypes and the collective unconscious, but as a clinician I am more interested in the phenomenology of archetypal experience rather than identifying the origins of archetypal patterns. In contrast to my earliest involvement with analytical psychology, I no longer hold on to assumptions about what an image from a dream or fantasy (e.g., house, horse, tree, mountain, etc.) might refer to. A week rarely passes in which I am not moved and amazed by the creativity, eloquence, and poetic nature of dreams, particularly when images emerge that capture so fully a pattern, theme, or situation which neither I nor my patient could have invented consciously.

In my practice, I rarely think in terms of Jung's typological theory unless one of my patients introduces it. Likewise, I have not found Jung's anima/animus theory useful to my practice or my understanding of patients. Nor do I administer the word association test to patients or try to teach my patients how to do active imagination. However, at pertinent junctures, I do suggest what I consider 'naturalistic' active imagination, often simply asking, "If you close your eyes for a moment, what comes into your awareness?" I find that presenting imaginal engagement in a less formal manner is more accessible to patients and often leads to greater access to imaginal reverie. Additionally, I do not suggest any of the ancillary expressive modalities mentioned in Chapter 9. However, some patients will occasionally bring expressive-creative work they've done to sessions or ask if I have materials they could draw with. In these respects, I am not a very traditional Jungian. I find that a focus on the primary modalities of dreamwork, analytic interaction, the use of the couch (when appropriate), interpretation, and the encouragement to speak whatever comes to mind (i.e., free association) provides sufficient conditions for the emergence of unconscious material, psychological growth, and ultimately transformation.

During my analytic journey there have been several statements from other authors that have found a home in my psyche and which filter into my thoughts on a routine basis: 1) The most central is a statement from the writer Aldous Huxley, "Experience is not what happens to a man; it is what a man does with what happens to him." This statement reminds me that the story a patient tells me is always inherently subjective, i.e., it reflects how the patient has internalized various historical events and relationships. Huxley's statement is in keeping with Spence's (1982) distinction between historical truth and narrative truth; 2) In terms of analytic goals or aims, a statement by the Spanish philosopher José Ortega y Gasset, "So many things fail to interest us, simply because they don't find in us enough surfaces on which to live, and what we have to do then is to increase the number of planes in our mind, so that a much larger number of themes can find a place in it at the same time." For me, Ortega y Gasset captures well one of the most essential aspects of the analytic process, i.e., the differentiation and complexification of one's relationship to the psyche and the expansion of the capacity for symbolic thought; 3) Muriel Dimen (2013, p. 61) indicates that "The psychoanalytic session is a chance to say the unspeakable and think the unthinkable. To imagine what does not yet exist." Although Dimen was a relational analyst, her statement outlines a crossroads between Jungian and Bionian perspectives, placing emphasis on the cultivation of imaginal capacity while also capturing the Bionian emphasis on 'negative capability' and non-representational experience; 4) and finally, from Gabbard and Ogden (2009, p. 322) a small meditation on the living responsibility of those practicing analysis, "With each patient, we have the responsibility to become an analyst whom we have never been before."

In my analytic training I was moved by Ghent's (1989) treatise "Credo" in which he outlines his movement from a one-person to a two-person psychoanalytic model and articulates with sensitivity and clarity the transformative elements of psychoanalysis as he sees it. Much of my writing and teaching has revolved around my own efforts to articulate what is central to my practice of analysis. While there are many more areas I could touch upon in terms of my practice as an analyst, these areas serve as an adequate introduction to some of the positions I practice from and how I perceive my relationship with analytical psychology as a contemporary Jungian psychoanalyst. The journey continues and the experience of living the analytic life continuously deepens. I am surprised by the many turns and opportunities that have arisen during the journey and I am grateful to the patients, students, supervisees, and colleagues who have trusted me to be involved with their journeys.

Conclusion

Developing Trends in Jungian Psychoanalysis

Previous chapters have described the current dialogue within analytical psychology around the integration of psychoanalytic approaches, neuroscience, archetypal theory, the concept of the collective unconscious, the cultural complex, and the anima/animus complex. However, several other hubs of conceptual attention have emerged over the past few decades. Because of the constraints on the length of this volume, I will only mention them here along with a few sample references for further consultation.

As described in earlier chapters, there are some conservative sectors in analytical psychology which would prefer to preserve the Jungian model just as it is presented in Jung's collected works. However, there is also an atmosphere of vibrant contemporary scholarship and reflection which is ongoing in the Jungian field. The main trends or areas of focus in the contemporary Jungian psychoanalytic community over the past several decades include:

1 new conceptualizations of the interaction between culture and psyche (Adams 1996; Kimbles 2000; Singer and Kimbles 2004);

2 contemporary Jungian perspectives on race (Brewster 2017, 2019; Brewster and Morgan 2021);

3 ecology and climate change (Foster 2011; Kiehl 2016; Merritt 2011, 2012a, 2012b);

4 somatic experience and embodiment (Sidoli 2000; Ramos 2004; Dunlea 2019);

DOI: 10.4324/9781003223511-12

5   activism, politics, and political violence (Kiehl, Saban, and Samuels 2016; Carta and Kiehl 2020; Singer 2021; Luci 2022);
6   refugees and immigration (Papadopoulos 2019, 2021; Tyminski 2022);
7   analytical psychology and science (Haule 2010a, 2010b);
8   gender, gender identity, sexuality, and sexual orientation (Downing 1991; Hopcke 1991; Hopcke, Carrington, and Wirth 1993; Kulkarni 1997; McKenzie 2006, 2010; Marsman 2017);
9   transgenerational trauma and transmission (Connolly 2011; Cavalli 2012; Kalinowska 2012); and
10 the impact of the global pandemic (Carpani and Luci 2022).

Final Reflections

My aim in this volume has been to provide a concise but comprehensive overview of Jung's model of psychoanalysis, to address some of the critiques of Jung's model, and to highlight some points of connection between Jung's model and other psychoanalytic orientations. Because my development and inclination have been towards the developmental and classical perspectives in analytical psychology, I can imagine that those more drawn to the work of Giegerich or the archetypal school who may not feel I have addressed those perspectives as fully as they deserve.

Contemporary Jungian psychoanalysis now incorporates many ideas from contemporary psychoanalysis, for example the concept of projective identification is widely utilized in Jungian psychoanalysis, although the concept originated with Melanie Klein. Jung adopted a similar concept, *participation mystique*, borrowed from the French anthropologist Lucien Lévy-Bruhl. However, while both terms describe a blurring of subject–object boundaries and unconscious to unconscious communication, the concept of *participation mystique* does not lend itself easily to clinical application because it does not address the psychological function underlying the experience. In contrast, the concept of projective identification more clearly describes the psychological purpose of the interaction in terms of defense and unconscious communication (Winborn 2014).

Similarly, contemporary psychoanalysis now includes many elements which were foreshadowed or explicitly articulated by Jung, but which Jung often addressed through metaphor, such as the alchemical metaphor, rather than through a more straightforward, theoretical development. For example, significant elements of the intersubjective and relational perspectives are anticipated in Jung's model of the analytic relationship and his transference discussion of the transference–countertransference matrix. Also, there is an emerging appreciation for spiritual, transcendent, and teleological experiences in contemporary psychoanalysis that has always been present in Jungian psychoanalysis. In general, Jungian psychoanalysis could benefit from the focus on technique and process found in many contemporary psychoanalytic orientations, while contemporary psychoanalysis would benefit from the strong emphasis placed on metaphor and the prospective elements of psychological experience that is found in Jungian psychoanalysis.

Fordham (1998) argued that psychoanalysis should be considered a 'fenceless field' in which ideas could interact freely and move fluidly, which brings us back full circle to Jung's observation, "Ultimate truth … requires the concert of many voices" (1976, ¶1236). In many respects, psychoanalysis of all forms is at a unique crossroads. On the one hand, there is greater empirical evidence for the efficacy of psychoanalytic therapy than ever before, as well as a tremendous degree of ancillary support for psychoanalytic theories emerging from neuroscience and cognitive science, as well as from research on primary affects, trauma, infant development, and attachment. However, psychoanalysis continues to come under attack or be dismissed by academia and insurance companies, as well as via distorted claims from competing therapies and companies vigorously promoting low-contact online and text-based substitutes for therapy. Additionally, the number of applicants for training in psychoanalysis has declined in many parts of the world, and the average age of the faculty of most training institutes has grown progressively older. In general, there are more threats and obstacles to the healthy continuation of psychoanalysis as a distinct and vibrant field than ever before. We live in a time in which the need for greater cooperation and respect between the various psychoanalytic orientations is needed more now than ever. We would do well to embrace our commonalities and cultivate curiosity about our differences. My hope is that this volume contributes to the ongoing rapprochement between analytical psychology and other psychoanalytic orientations, so that all forms of psychoanalysis, including Jungian psychoanalysis, can co-exist and flourish under one pluralistic roof.

Bibliography

Adams, M.V. (1996). *The Multicultural Imagination: 'Race', Color and the Unconscious*. London: Routledge.

Adler, G. (1967). *Studies in Analytical Psychology*. New York: Putnam.

Alvarez, A. (1992). *Live Company: Psychoanalytic Psychotherapy with Autistic, Borderline, Deprived and Abused Children*. London: Routledge.

Astor, J. (1995). *Michael Fordham: Innovations in Analytical Psychology*. London: Routledge.

Astor, J. (2002). Analytical psychology and its relation to psychoanalysis: A personal view. *J. Anal. Psych.*, 47: 599–612.

Astor, J. (2011). Saying what you mean, meaning what you say: Language, interaction and interpretation. *J. Anal. Psychol.*, 5: 203–216.

Atwood, G. and Stolorow, R. (1979). *Faces in a Cloud: Intersubjectivity and Personality Theory*. Northvale, NJ: Aronson.

Bacal, H. (2011). *The Power of Specificity in Psychotherapy*. Lanham, MD: Rowman & Littlefield.

Barsness, R. (Ed.) (2018). *Core Competencies of Relational Psychoanalysis: A Guide to Practice, Study, and Research*. London: Routledge.

Beebe, J., Cambray, J., and Kirsch, T.B. (2001). What Freudians can learn from Jung. *Psychoanalytic Psychology*, 18: 213–242.

Beebe, B. and Lachmann, F. (2002). *Infant Research and Adult Treatment*. Mahwah, NJ: Lawrence Erlbaum.

Berry, P. (1982). *Echo's Subtle Body: Contributions to an Archetypal Psychology*. Dallas, TX: Spring Publications.

Bion, W.R. (1959). Attacks on linking. *Inter. J. of Psychoanalysis*, 40: 308–315.

Bion, W.R. (1962/1983). *Learning from Experience*. New York and London: Aronson.

Bion, W.R. (1965). *Transformations*. Northvale, NJ: Aronson.

Bion, W.R. (1970/1983). *Attention and Interpretation*. Northvale, NJ: Aronson.

Bion, W.R. (1983). *Elements of Psycho-analysis*. Northvale, NJ: Aronson.

Bion, W.R. (1990). *Brazilian Seminars*. London: Karnac.

Bion, W.R. (1993). *Second Thoughts*. London: Karnac.

Bion, W.R. (1994). *Clinical Seminars and Other Works*. London: Karnac.

Bisagni, F. (2013). On the impact of words: Interpretation, empathy and affect regulation. *J. Anal. Psychol.*, 58: 615–635.

Bisagni, F. (2019). *Obsessions: The Twisted Cruelty*. London: Routledge.

Blue, D. and Harrang, C. (2016). *From Reverie to Interpretation: Transforming Thought into the Action of Psychoanalysis*. London: Karnac.

Bosnak, R. (1986). *Tracks in the Wilderness of Dreaming*. New York: Delacorte Press.

Bovensiepen, G. (2002). Symbolic attitude and reverie. *J. Anal. Psychol.*, 47: 241–257.

Bovensiepen, G. (2006). Attachment-dissociation network: Some thoughts about a modern complex theory. *J. Anal. Psychol.*, 51: 451–466.

Braun, C. (2020). *The Therapeutic Relationship in Analytical Psychology: Theory and Practice*. London: Routledge.

Brewster, F. (2017). *African Americans and Jungian Psychology: Leaving the Shadows*. London: Routledge.

Brewster, F. (2019). *The Racial Complex: A Jungian Perspective on Culture and Race*. London: Routledge.

Brewster, F. and Morgan, H. (2021). *Racial Legacies: Jung, Politics and Culture*. London: Routledge.

Brooke, R. (2000). *Pathways into the Jungian World: Phenomenology and Analytical Psychology*. London: Routledge.

Brooke, R. (2015). *Jung and Phenomenology: Classic Edition*. London: Routledge.

Brown, R.S. (Ed.) (2018). *Re-encountering Jung: Analytical Psychology and Contemporary Psychoanalysis*. London: Routledge.

Campbell, J. (1949). *The Hero with a Thousand Faces*. Princeton, NJ: Princeton University Press.

Caropreso, F. (2017). The death instinct and the mental dimension beyond the pleasure principle in the works of Spielrein and Freud. *Int. J. Psycho-Anal.*, 98: 1741–1762.

Carotenuto, A. (1992). *The Difficult Art: A Critical Discourse on Psychotherapy*. Wilmette, IL: Chiron.

Carpani, S. and Luci, M. (Eds.) (2022). *Lockdown Therapy: Reflections on How the Pandemic Changed Psychotherapy*. London: Routledge.

Carta, S. and Kiehl, E. (Eds.) (2020). *Political Passions and Jungian Psychology: Social and Political Activism in Analysis*. London: Routledge.

Carvalho, R. (2014). Synchronicity, the infinite unrepressed, dissociation and the interpersonal. *J. Anal. Psychol.*, 59: 366–384.

Casement, A. (2011). The interiorizing movement of logical life: Reflections on Wolfgang Giegerich. *J. Anal. Psychol.*, 56: 532–549.

Cavalli, A. (2012). Transgenerational transmission of indigestible facts: From trauma, deadly ghosts and mental voids to meaning-making interpretations. *J. Anal. Psychol.*, 57: 597–614.

Charlton, R.S. (1986). Free association and Jungian analytic technique. *J. Anal. Psychol.*, 31: 153–171.

Charlton, R.S. (1997). Fictions of the internal object. *J. Anal. Psychol.*, 42: 81–97.

Chodorow, J. (1991). *Dance Therapy and Depth Psychology: The Moving Imagination*. London: Routledge.

Civitarese, G. (2015). *The Necessary Dream: New Theories and Techniques of Interpretation in Psychoanalysis*. London: Karnac.

Civitarese, G. & Ferro, A. (2013). The meaning and use of metaphor in analytic field theory. *Psychoanalytic Inquiry*, 33: 190–209.

Colman, W. (2007). Symbolic conceptions: The idea of the third. *J. Anal. Psychol.*, 52: 565–583.

Colman, W. (2013). Bringing it all back home: How I became a relational analyst. *J. Anal. Psychol.*, 58: 470–490.

Colman, W. (2021). *Act and Image: The Emergence of Symbolic Imagination*. London: Routledge.

Connolly, A. (2011). Healing the wounds of our fathers: Intergenerational trauma, memory, symbolization and narrative. *J. Anal. Psychol.*, 56: 607–626.

Corbett, L. (2020). Is the Self other to the Self? Why does the numinosum feel like another? The relevance of Matte Blanco to our understanding of the unconscious. *J. Anal. Psychol.*, 65: 672–684.

Covington, C. (1995). No story, no analysis? The role of narrative in interpretation. *J. Anal. Psychol.*, 40: 405–417.

Cowan, L. (1982). *Masochism: A Jungian View*. Dallas, TX: Spring Publications.

Culbert-Koehn, J. (1997). Between Bion and Jung: A talk with James Grotstein. *The San Francisco Jung Inst. Library J.*, 15 (4): 15–32.

Culbert-Koehn, J. (2000). Classical Jung meets Klein and Bion. *Psychoanal. Dial.*, 10: 443–455.

Cwik, A. (2011). Associative dreaming: Reverie and imagination. *J. Anal. Psychol.*, 56: 14–36.

Cwik, A. (2017). What is a Jungian analyst dreaming when myth comes to mind? Thirdness as an aspect of the anima media natura. *J. Anal. Psychol.*, 62: 107–129.

Davidson, D. (1966). Transference as a form of active imagination. *J. Anal. Psychol.*, 11: 135–146.

Dehing, J. (1992). The therapist's interventions in Jungian analysis. *J. Anal. Psychol.*, 37: 29–47.

Dieckmann, H. (1991). *Methods in Analytical Psychology: An Introduction*. Wilmette, IL: Chiron.

Dieckmann, H. (1999). *Complexes: Diagnosis and Therapy in Analytical Psychology*. Wilmette, IL: Chiron.

Dieterich, A. (1910). *Eine Mithrasliturgie*. Leipzig and Berlin: Teubner.

Dimen, M. (2013). *Sexuality, Intimacy, Power*. New York and London: Routledge.

Dougherty, N. and West, J. (2007). *The Matrix and Meaning of Character*. London: Routledge.

Downing, C. (1991). *Myths and Mysteries of Same-Sex Love*. New York: Continuum.

Dunlea, M. (2019). *Bodydreaming in the Treatment of Developmental Trauma*. London: Routledge.

Edinger, E. (1984). *The Creation of Consciousness: Jung's Myth for Modern Man*. Toronto: Inner City Books.

Edinger, E. (1985). *Anatomy of the Psyche: Alchemical Symbolism in Psychotherapy*. La Salle, IL: Open Court.

Edinger, E. (1994). *The Eternal Drama: The Inner Meaning of Greek Mythology*. Boston, MA: Shambhala.

Eisold, K. (2002). Jung, Jungians, and psychoanalysis. *Psychoanal. Psychol.*, 19 (3): 501–524.

Ellenberger, H. (1970). *The Discovery of the Unconscious: The History and Evolution of Dynamic Psychiatry*. New York: Basic Books.

Escamilla, M., Sandoval, H., Calhoun, V., and Ramirez, M. (2018). Brain activation patterns in response to complex triggers in the word association test: Results from a new study in the United States. *J. Anal. Psychol.*, 63: 484–509.

Etchegoyen, R.H. (2005). *Fundamentals of Psychoanalytic Technique*. London: Karnac.

Fenichel, O. (1941). *Problems of Psychoanalytic Technique*. New York: The Psychoanalytic Quarterly.

Field, N. (1994). Object relations and individuation: Are they complementary or in conflict? *J. Anal. Psychol.*, 39: 463–478.

Fonagy, P. (1991). Thinking about thinking: Some clinical and theoretical considerations in the treatment of a borderline patient. *Int. J. Psycho-Anal.*, 72: 639–656.

Fonagy, P. (2000). Attachment and borderline personality disorder. *J. Amer. Psychoanal. Assn.*, 48: 1129–1146.

Fordham, M. (1971). Primary self, primary narcissism and related concepts. *J. Anal. Psychol.*, 16: 168–182.

Fordham, M. (1974). Defences of the Self. *J. Anal. Psychol.*, 19 (2): 192–199.

Fordham, M. (1978). *Jungian Psychotherapy: A Study in Analytical Psychology.* London: Karnac.

Fordham, M. (1979). Analytical psychology and countertransference. *Contemporary Psychoanalysis*, 15: 630–646.

Fordham, M. (1985). *Explorations into the Self.* London: Karnac.

Fordham, M. (1991a). The supposed limits of interpretation. *J. Anal. Psychol.*, 36: 165–175.

Fordham, M. (1991b). Rejoinder to Nathan Schwartz-Salant. *J. Anal. Psychol.*, 36: 367–369.

Fordham, M. (1993). *The Making of an Analyst: A Memoir.* London: Free Association.

Fordham, M. (1994). *Children as Individuals* (revised version of a book originally published in 1944 as *The Life of Childhood*). London: Free Association.

Fordham, M. (1998). *Freud, Jung, Klein: The Fenceless Field.* London: Routledge.

Fordham, M., Gordon, R., Hubback, J., and Lambert, K. (1978). *Technique in Jungian Analysis.* London: Karnac.

Fosshage, J.L. (1994). Toward reconceptualising transference: Theoretical and clinical considerations. *Int. J. Psycho-Anal.*, 75: 265–280.

Foster, S. (2011). *Risky Business.* Toronto: Inner City Books.

Freud, S. (1899/1955). *The Interpretation of Dreams.* New York: Basic Books.

Freud, S. (1913). Totem and taboo. *SE13*: 1–161.

Freud, S. (1914). Remembering, repeating and working through. *SE12*: 145–156.

Freud, S. (1939). Moses and monotheism. *SE23*: 7–137.

Freud, S. (1959). *Collected Papers – Volume II: Clinical Papers and Papers on Technique.* New York: Basic Books.

Freud, S., and Breuer, J. (1895/2004). *Studies in Hysteria.* Trans. N. Luckhurst. New York: Penguin.

Gabbard, G. and Ogden, T. (2009). On becoming a psychoanalyst. *Int. J. Psycho-Anal.*, 90: 311–327.

Garcia, E. (1988). In the beginning … phylogeny in Freud's overview of the transference neuroses: A review-essay. *Jefferson J. of Psychiatry*, 6 (2): 89–99.

Ghent, E. (1989). Credo: The dialectics of one-person and two-person psychologies. *Contemporary Psychoanalysis*, 25: 169–211.

Giegerich, W. (1998). *The Soul's Logical Life*. Bern, Switzerland: Peter Lang.

Giegerich, W. (2005). *The Collected English Papers, Vol. 1: The Neurosis of Psychology: Primary Papers toward a Critical Psychology*. New Orleans: Spring Journal Books.

Giegerich, W. (2008). *The Collected English Papers, Vol. 3: Soul-Violence*. New Orleans: Spring Journal Books.

Giegerich, W. (2010). *The Collected English Papers, Vol. 4: The Soul Always Thinks*. New Orleans: Spring Journal Books.

Giegerich, W. (2012). *What is Soul?* New Orleans: Spring Journal Books.

Goodwyn, E. (2021). Archetypal origins: Biology vs culture is a false dichotomy. *Int. J. of Jungian Studies*, 13: 111–129.

Gordon, K. (2004). The tiger's stripe: Some thoughts on psychoanalysis, gnosis, and the experience of wonderment. *Contemp. Psychoanal.*, 40, 5–45.

Gordon, R. (1985). Big Self and little self: Some reflections. *J. Anal. Psychol.*, 30: 261–271.

Greene, L. (2018). *Jung's Studies in Astrology: Prophecy, Magic, and the Qualities of Time*. London: Routledge.

Greenson, R. (1967). *The Technique and Practice of Psychoanalysis*. Madison, CT: International Universities Press.

Groden, M. and Kreiswirth, M. (Eds.) (1994). *The Johns Hopkins Guide to Literary Theory and Criticism*. Baltimore, MD: Johns Hopkins University Press.

Groesbeck, C.J. (1975). The archetypal image of the wounded healer. *J. Anal. Psychol.*, 20: 122–145.

Grosskurth, P. (1991). *The Secret Ring: Freud's Inner Circle and the Politics of Psychoanalysis*. New York: Addison-Wesley.

Grotstein, J. (2000). *Who is the Dreamer Who Dreams the Dream? A Study of Psychic Presences*. London: Routledge.

Grotstein, J. (2007). *A Beam of Intense Darkness: Wilfred Bion's Legacy to Psychoanalysis*. London: Routledge.

Grubrich-Simitis, I. (1987). *A Phylogenetic Fantasy: Overview of the Transference Neuroses*. Cambridge, MA: Harvard University Press.

Gudaitè, G. and Kelly, T. (Eds.) (2022). *Exploring Core Competencies in Jungian Psychoanalysis: Research, Practice, and Training*. London: Routledge.

Guggenbühl-Craig, A. (1971). *Power in the Helping Professions*. Dallas, TX: Spring Publications.

Hall, J. (1983). *Jungian Dream Interpretation: A Handbook of Theory and Practice*. Toronto: Inner City Books.

Hannah, B. (1981). *Encounters with the Soul: Active Imagination as Developed by C.G. Jung*. Boston, MA: Sigo Press.

Harding, M.E. (1963). *Psychic Energy: Its Source and Its Transformation*. Princeton, NJ: Princeton University Press.

Haule, J. (2010a). *Jung in the 21st Century, Volume One: Evolution and Archetype*. London: Routledge.

Haule, J. (2010b). *Jung in the 21st Century, Volume Two: Synchronicity and Science*. London: Routledge.

Hillman, J. (1977). An inquiry into image. *Spring Journal*, 62–88.

Hillman, J. (1978). Further notes on images. *Spring Journal*, 152–182.

Hillman, J. (1979a). *The Dream and the Underworld*. New York: Harper & Row.

Hillman, J. (1979b). Image-sense. *Spring Journal*, 130–143.

Hillman, J. (1980). *Facing the Gods*. Dallas, TX: Spring Publications.

Hillman, J. (1981). *The Thought of the Heart*. Dallas, TX: Spring Publications.

Hillman, J. (1983). *Archetypal Psychology: A Brief Account*. Dallas, TX: Spring Publications.

Hillman, J. (1989). *A Blue Fire*. New York: Harper & Row.

Hoffer, P.T. (1992). The concept of phylogenetic inheritance in Freud and Jung. *J. of the Amer. Psychoanalytic Assoc.*, 40: 517–530.

Hogenson, G.B. (2009). Archetypes as action patterns. *J. Anal. Psychol.*, 54: 325–337.

Hogenson, G.B. (2019). The controversy around the concept of archetypes. *J. Anal. Psychol.*, 64: 682–700.

Hopcke, R. (1991). *Jung, Jungians, and Homosexuality*. Boston, MA: Shambhala.

Hopcke, R.H., Carrington, K.L., and Wirth, S. (Eds.) (1993). *Same-Sex Love and the Path to Wholeness*. Boston, MA: Shambhala.

Hunter, V. (1994). *Psychoanalysts Talk*. New York: Guilford.

Isaacs, S. (1948). The nature and function of phantasy. *Int. J. Psycho-Anal.*, 29: 73–97.

Jacobi, J. (1973). *The Psychology of C.G. Jung*. New Haven, CT: Yale University Press.

Jacobson, E. (1964). *The Self and the Object World*. New York: International Universities Press.

Jacoby, M. (1984). *The Analytic Encounter: Transference and Human Relationship*. Toronto: Inner City Books.

Jacoby, M. (1990). *Individuation and Narcissism: The Psychology of Self in Jung and Kohut*. London: Routledge.

Jacoby, M. (1999). *Jungian Psychotherapy and Contemporary Infant Research: Basic Patterns of Emotional Exchange.* London: Routledge.

Johansson, P.M. and Punzi, E. (2019). Jewishness and psychoanalysis: The relationship to identity, trauma and exile. An interview study. *Jewish Culture and History*, 20 (2): 140–152.

Jung, C.G. (1911). On the doctrine of complexes. In *CW2*. Princeton, NJ: Princeton University Press.

Jung, C.G. (1912/1991). *Psychology of the Unconscious: A Study of the Transformations and Symbolisms of the Libido. CWB.* Princeton, NJ: Princeton University Press.

Jung, C.G. (1916/1928). The structure of the unconscious. In *CW7*. Princeton, NJ: Princeton University Press.

Jung, C.G. (1916/1948). General aspects of dream psychology. In *CW8*. Princeton, NJ: Princeton University Press.

Jung, C.G. (1917). On the psychology of the unconscious. In *CW7*. Princeton, NJ: Princeton University Press.

Jung, C.G. (1919). Instinct and the unconscious. In *CW8*. Princeton, NJ: Princeton University Press.

Jung, C.G. (1931a). Mind and earth. In *CW10*. Princeton, NJ: Princeton University Press.

Jung, C.G. (1931b). The structure of the psyche. In *CW8*. Princeton, NJ: Princeton University Press.

Jung, C.G. (1931/1934). The practical use of dream-analysis. In *CW16*. Princeton, NY: Princeton University Press.

Jung, C.G. (1933). *Modern Man in Search of a Soul.* New York: Harcourt Brace Jovanovich.

Jung, C.G. (1934). Picasso. In *CW15*. Princeton, NJ: Princeton University Press.

Jung, C.G. (1934/1954). Archetypes of the collective unconscious. In *CW9i*. Princeton, NJ: Princeton University Press.

Jung, C.G. (1935). The Tavistock lectures. In *CW18*. Princeton, NJ: Princeton University Press.

Jung, C.G. (1936). On the concept of the collective unconscious. In *CW9i*. Princeton, NY: Princeton University Press.

Jung, C.G. (1936/1937). Psychological factors in human behavior. In *CW8*. Princeton, NJ: Princeton University Press.

Jung, C.G. (1945). Medicine and psychotherapy. In *CW16*. Princeton, NY: Princeton University Press.

Jung, C.G. (1945/1948). On the nature of dreams. In *CW8*. Princeton, NJ: Princeton University Press.

Jung, C.G. (1945/1954). The philosophical tree. In *CW13*. Princeton, NJ: Princeton University Press.

Jung, C.G. (1946). The psychology of the transference. In *CW16*. Princeton, NY: Princeton University Press.

Jung, C.G. (1948a). A psychological approach to the dogma of the trinity. In *CW11*. Princeton, NY: Princeton University Press.

Jung, C.G. (1948b). A review of the complex theory. In *CW8*. Princeton, NJ: Princeton University Press.

Jung, C.G. (1948c). On psychic energy. In *CW8*. Princeton, NJ: Princeton University Press.

Jung, C.G. (1950). Flying saucers: A modern myth. In *CW10*. Princeton, NJ: Princeton University Press.

Jung, C.G. (1951). The psychology of the child archetype. In *CW9i*. Princeton, NJ: Princeton University Press.

Jung, C.G. (1952a). Synchronicity: An acausal connecting principle. In *CW8*. Princeton, NJ: Princeton University Press.

Jung, C.G. (1952b). Answer to Job. In *CW11*. Princeton, NJ: Princeton University Press.

Jung, C.G. (1954a). Concerning the archetypes, with special reference to the anima concept. In *CW9i*. Princeton, NJ: Princeton University Press.

Jung, C.G. (1954b). On the nature of the psyche. In *CW8*. Princeton, NJ: Princeton University Press.

Jung, C.G. (1954/1966). The practice of psychotherapy. In *CW16*. Princeton, NJ: Princeton University Press.

Jung, C.G. (1956). Symbols of transformation. In *CW5*. Princeton, NJ: Princeton University Press.

Jung, C.G. (1956/1963). Mysterium Coniunctionis. In *CW14*. Princeton, NJ: Princeton University Press.

Jung, C.G. (1958). The transcendent function. In *CW8*. Princeton, NJ: Princeton University Press.

Jung, C.G. (1959). Aion: Researches into the phenomenology of the self. In *CW9ii*. Princeton, NJ: Princeton University Press.

Jung, C.G. (1959/1969). The Archetypes and the Collective Unconscious. In *CW9i*. Princeton, NJ: Princeton University Press.

Jung, C.G. (1960). The Psychogenesis of Mental Disease. In *CW3*. Princeton, NJ: Princeton University Press.

Jung, C.G. (1960/1969). The Structure and Dynamics of the Psyche. In *CW8*. Princeton, NJ: Princeton University Press.

Jung, C.G. (Ed.) (1964). *Man and His Symbols*. New York: Dell.

Jung, C.G. (1965). *Memories, Dreams, Reflections*. New York: Vintage.

Jung, C.G. (1966). Two Essays on Analytical Psychology. In *CW7*. Princeton, NJ: Princeton University Press.

Jung, C.G. (1967). Alchemical Studies. In *CW13*. Princeton, NJ: Princeton University Press.

Jung, C.G. (1968). Psychology and Alchemy. In *CW12*. Princeton, NJ: Princeton University Press.

Jung, C.G. (1969). Archetypes of the Collective Unconscious. In *CW9i*. Princeton, NJ: Princeton University Press.

Jung, C.G. (1971). Psychological Types. In *CW6*. Princeton, NJ: Princeton University Press.

Jung, C.G. (1973a). Experimental Researches. In *CW2*. Princeton, NJ: Princeton University Press.

Jung, C.G. (1973b). *Letters*, Vol. 1. Princeton, NJ: Princeton University Press.

Jung, C.G. (1976). The Symbolic Life. In *CW18*. Princeton, NJ: Princeton University Press.

Jung, C.G. (1977). *C.G. Jung Speaking: Interviews and Encounters*. Princeton, NJ: Princeton University Press.

Jung, C.G. (2008). *Children's Dreams: Notes from the Seminar Given in 1936–1940. CW Supplemental Volume*. Princeton, NJ: Princeton University Press.

Jung, C.G. (2009). *The Red Book: Liber Novus*. New York: W.W. Norton.

Jung, C.G. (2020). *The Black Books of C.G. Jung* (7 volumes). S. Shamdasani (Ed.). Translated by M. Liebscher, J. Peck, and S. Shamdasani. New York: Philemon Series and W.W. Norton & Co.

Jung, C.G. and Kerenyi, C. (1949). *Essays on a Science of Mythology*. New York: Harper.

Kalinowska, M. (2012). Monuments of memory: Defensive mechanisms of the collective psyche and their manifestation in the memorialization process. *J. Anal. Psychol.*, 57: 425–444.

Kalsched, D. (1996). *The Inner World of Trauma and Soul: A Psycho-Spiritual Approach to Human Development and Its Interruption*. London: Routledge.

Kalsched, D. (2010). *Defenses in dreams: Clinical reflections on the multiplicity necessary for survival in pieces*. Paper given at 18th IAAP Congress in Montreal, August 27, 2010.

Kalsched, D. (2013). *Trauma and Soul: A Psycho-Spiritual Approach to Human Development and its Interruption*. London: Routledge.

Kalsched, D. (2015). Revisioning Fordham's 'Defences of the Self' in light of modern relational theory and contemporary neuroscience. *J. Anal. Psychol.*, 60: 477–496.

Karbelnig, A. M. (2020). The theater of the unconscious mind. *Psycho-analytic Psychology.*, 37: 273–281.

Kast, V. (1993). *Imagination as Space of Freedom: Dialogue between the Ego and the Unconscious.* New York: Fromm International.

Kast, V. (1996) The clinical use of fairy tales by a 'classical' Jungian analyst. *Psychoanal. Rev.*, 83: 509–523.

Kiehl, J. (2016). *Facing Climate Change: An Integrated Path to the Future.* New York: Columbia University Press.

Kiehl, E., Saban, M., and Samuels, A. (Eds.) (2016). *Analysis and Activism: Social and Political Contributions of Jungian Psychology.* London: Routledge.

Kimbles, S. (2000). Cultural complexes and the myth of invisibility. In T. Singer (Ed.), *The Vision Thing.* New York: Routledge.

Kirsch, T. (2000). *The Jungians: A Comparative and Historical Perspective.* London: Routledge.

Klein, M. (1935). A contribution to the psychogenesis of manic-depressive states. *Int. J. Psycho-Anal.*, 16: 145–174.

Klein, M. (1952). The mutual influences in the development of ego and id. *Psychoanalytic Study of the Child*, 7: 51–53.

Knox, J. (1997). Internal objects. *J. Anal. Psychol.*, 42 (4): 653–666.

Knox, J. (2001). Memories, fantasies, archetypes: An exploration of some connections between cognitive science and analytical psychology. *J. Anal. Psychol.*, 46: 613–635.

Knox, J. (2003). *Archetype, Attachment, Analysis: Jungian Psychology and the Emergent Mind.* London: Brunner-Routledge.

Knox, J. (2004). From archetypes to reflective function. *J. Anal. Psychol.*, 49: 1–19.

Knox, J. (2007). Who owns the unconscious? Or why psychoanalysts need to 'own' Jung. In A. Casement (Ed.), *Who Owns Jung?* London: Karnac.

Knox, J. (2011). *Self-Agency in Psychotherapy: Attachment, Autonomy, and Intimacy.* New York: W.W. Norton.

Kohut, H. (1977). *The Restoration of the Self.* Madison, CT: International Universities Press.

Kohut, H. (1984). *How Does Analysis Cure?* Chicago, IL: University of Chicago Press.

Krieger, N.M. (2019). A dynamic systems approach to the feeling toned complex. *J. Anal. Psychol.*, 64: 738–760.

Kroeker, J. (2019). *Jungian Music Psychotherapy: When Psyche Sings.* London: Routledge.

Kulkarni, C. (1997). *Lesbians and Lesbianisms: A Post-Jungian Perspective.* London: Routledge.

Ledermann, R. (1995). Thoughts on interpreting. *J. Anal. Psychol.*, 40: 523–529.

Luci, M. (2022). *Torture Survivors in Analytic Therapy: Jung, Politics, Culture*. London: Routledge.

Maier, C. (2014). Intersubjectivity and the creation of meaning in the analytic process. *J. Anal. Psychol.*, 59: 624–640.

Marsman, M.A. (2017). Transgenderism and transformation: An attempt at a Jungian understanding. *J. Anal. Psychol.*, 62: 678–687.

McDougall, J. (1985). *Theaters of the Body: A Psychoanalytic Approach to Psychosomatic Illness*. New York: Brunner/Mazel.

McDougall, J. (1989). *Theaters of the Mind: Illusion and Truth on the Psychoanalytic Stage*. New York: Brunner/Mazel.

McGuire, W. (Ed.) (1974). *The Freud/Jung Letters: The Correspondence between Sigmund Freud and C.G. Jung*. Cambridge, MA: Harvard University Press.

McKenzie, S. (2006). Queering gender: Anima/animus and the paradigm of emergence. *J. Anal. Psychol.*, 51: 401–421.

McKenzie, S. (2010). Genders and sexualities in individuation: Theoretical and clinical explorations. *J. Anal. Psychol.*, 55: 91–111.

McWilliams, N. (1994). *Psychoanalytic Diagnosis: Understanding Personality Structures in Clinical Process*. New York: Guilford.

Merchant, J. (2006). The developmental/emergent model of archetype, its implications, and its application to shamanism. *J. Anal. Psychol.*, 51: 125–144.

Merchant, J. (2009). A reappraisal of classical archetype theory and its implications for theory and practice. *J. Anal. Psychol.*, 54: 339–358.

Merriam-Webster (n.d.). Merriam-Webster online dictionary. Retrieved from https://www.merriam-webster.com/dictionary/hermeneutics.

Merritt, D.L. (2011). *Jung and Ecopsychology: The Diary Farmer's Guide to the Universe*. Skiatook, OK: Fisher King Press.

Merritt, D.L. (2012a). *Hermes, Ecopsychology, and Complexity Theory*. Skiatook, OK: Fisher King Press.

Merritt, D.L. (2012b). *The Cry of Merlin: Jung, The Prototypical Ecopsychologist*. Skiatook, OK: Fisher King Press.

Mills J. (2018). The myth of the collective unconscious. *J. Hist. Behav.*, 55 (1): 1–14.

Mitchell, S. and Black, M. (1995). *Freud and Beyond: A History of Modern Psychoanalytic Thought*. New York: Basic Books.

Murdock, M. (1990). *The Heroine's Journey: Woman's Quest for Wholeness*. Boston, MA: Shambhala.

Neumann, E. (1966). Narcissism, normal self-formulation, and the primary relation to the mother. *Spring Journal*, 81–106.

Neumann, E. (1972). *The Great Mother: An Analysis of the Archetype*. Princeton, NJ: Princeton University Press.

Newirth, J. (2003). *Between Emotion and Cognition: The Generative Unconscious*. New York: Other Press.

Ogden, T. (1994). *Subjects of Analysis*. Northvale, NJ: Aronson.

Ogden, T. (2004). The analytic third: Implications for psychoanalytic theory and technique. *Psychoanal. Q.*, 73 (1): 167–195.

Ogden, T. (2017). Dreaming the analytic session: A clinical essay. *Psychoanalytic Quarterly.*, 86: 1–20.

Oremland, J. (1991). *Interpretation and Interaction: Psychoanalysis or Psychotherapy?*Hillsdale, NJ: Analytic Press.

Otto, R. (1923/1965). *The Idea of the Holy*. New York: Oxford University Press.

Papadopoulos, R. (2019). *Therapeutic Care for Refugees: No Place like Home*. London: Routledge.

Papadopoulos, R. (2021). *Involuntary Dislocation: Home, Trauma, Resilience, and Adversity-Activated Development*. London: Routledge.

Plaut, A. (1974). Part-object relations and Jung's 'luminosities'. *J. Anal. Psychol.*, 19: 165–181.

Plaut, A. (1975). Object constancy or constant object? *J. Anal. Psychol.*, 20: 207–215.

Quinodoz, D. (2003). *Words that Touch: A Psychoanalyst Learns to Speak*. P. Slotkin (trans.). London: Karnac.

Ramos, D. (2004). *The Psyche of the Body: A Jungian Approach to Psychosomatics*. London: Brunner-Routledge.

Reagan, A.J., Mitchell, L., Kiley, D., et al. (2016). The emotional arcs of stories are dominated by six basic shapes. *EPJ Data Sci.*, 5 (31): 1–8.

Redfearn, J.W. (1985). *My Self, My Many Selves*. London: Academic Press.

Redfearn, J.W. (1994). Introducing subpersonality theory. *J. Anal. Psychol.*, 39: 283–309.

Roazen, P. (1976). *Freud and His Followers*. London: Penguin.

Roesler, C. (2019). Theoretical foundations of analytical psychology: Recent developments and controversies. *J. Anal. Psychol.*, 64: 658–681.

Roesler, C. (2020). Jungian theory of dreaming and contemporary dream research: Findings from the research project 'Structural Dream Analysis'. *J. Anal. Psychol.*, 65: 44–62.

Roesler, C. (2022). *C.G. Jung's Archetype Concept: Theory, Research and Applications*. London: Routledge.

Roesler, C. and van Uffelen, T. (2018). Complexes and the unconscious: From the association experiment to recent fMRI studies. In C. Roesler, *Research in Analytical Psychology: Empirical Research*. London: Routledge.

Rosegrant, J. (2012). Why Bion? Why Jung? For that matter, why Freud? *J. Amer. Psychoanal. Assn.*, 60: 721–745.

Rubovits-Seitz, P. (2002). The fate of interpretation in postclassical schools of psychoanalysis. *Psychoanalysis and Contemp. Thought*, 25: 363–432.

Safran, J.D. (2006). The relational unconscious, the enchanted interior, and the return of the repressed. *Contemp. Psychoanal.*, 42: 393–412.

Samuels, A. (1985). *Jung and the Post-Jungians*. London: Routledge.

Samuels, A. (1989). *The Plural Psyche: Personality, Morality and the Father*. London: Routledge.

Samuels, A. (Ed.) (1991). *Psychopathology: Contemporary Jungian Perspectives*. New York: Guilford.

Samuels, A. (1996). Jung's return from banishment. *Psychoanal. Rev.*, 83: 469–489.

Samuels, A. (2000). Post-Jungian dialogues. *Psychoanalytic Dialogues*, 10: 403–426.

Samuels, A., Shorter, B., and Plaut, F. (1986). *A Critical Dictionary of Jungian Analysis*. London: Routledge.

Sandler, J. and Dreher, A. (1996). *What Do Psychoanalysts Want? The Problem of Aims in Psychoanalytic Therapy*. London: Routledge.

Scharff, D. and Scharff, J. (1992). *Scharff Notes: A Primer of Object Relations Therapy*. Northvale, NJ: Aronson.

Schaverien, J. (2007). Countertransference as active imagination: Imaginative experiences of the analyst. *J. Anal. Psychol.*, 52: 413–431.

Schwartz-Salant, N. (1982). *Narcissism and Character Transformation: The Psychology of Narcissistic Character Disorders*. Toronto: Inner City Books.

Schwartz-Salant, N. (1989). *The Borderline Personality: Vision and Healing*. Wilmette, IL: Chiron.

Schwartz-Salant, N. (1991). Vision, interpretation, and the interactive field. *J. Anal. Psychol.*, 36: 343–365.

Schwartz-Salant, N. (1992). Anima and animus in Jung's alchemical mirror. In N. Schwartz-Salant and M. Stein (Eds.), *Gender and Soul in Psychotherapy* (pp. 1–23). Wilmette, IL: Chiron.

Schwartz-Salant, N. (1995). On the interactive field as the analytic object. In N. Schwartz-Salant (Ed.), *The Interactive Field in Analysis*. Wilmette, IL: Chiron.

Sedgwick, D. (1993). *Jung and Searles: A Comparative Study.* London: Routledge.

Sedgwick, D. (1994). *The Wounded Healer: Countertransference from a Jungian Perspective.* London: Routledge.

Sedgwick, D. (2001). *Introduction to Jungian Psychotherapy: The Therapeutic Relationship.* Brighton: Brunner-Routledge.

Sedgwick, D. (2012). *Jung as a pioneer of relational analysis.* Paper presented at the 10th Anniversary Conference of the International Association for Relational Psychotherapy and Psychoanalysis (IARPP) in New York, March, 2012

Shalit, E. (2002). *The Complex: Path of Transformation from Archetype to Ego.* Toronto: Inner City Books.

Sharp, D. (1991). *C.G. Jung Lexicon.* Toronto: Inner City Books.

Shearer, A. (2004). On the making of myths: Mythology in training. *J. of Jungian Theory and Practice,* 6 (2): 1–14.

Sidoli, M. (2000). *The Body Speaks: The Archetypes in the Body.* London: Routledge.

Siegelman, E. (1990). *Metaphor and Meaning in Psychotherapy.* New York: Guilford.

Siegelman, E. (1994). Reframing 'reductive' analysis. *J. Anal. Psychol.,* 39: 479–496.

Singer, T. (2021). *From Vision to Folly in the American Soul: Jung, Politics and Culture.* London: Routledge.

Singer, T. and Kimbles, S. (2004). *The Cultural Complex: Contemporary Jungian Perspectives on Psyche and Society.* London: Routledge.

Solomon, H.M. (1991). Archetypal psychology and object relations theory. *J. Anal. Psychol.,* 36: 307–329.

Spence, D. (1982). *Narrative Truth and Historical Truth: Meaning and Interpretation in Psychoanalysis.* New York: W.W. Norton.

Spielrein, S. (1912/1994). Destruction as the cause of coming into being. *J. Anal. Psychol.,* 39: 155–186.

Stein, L. (1967). Introducing not-Self. *J. Anal. Psychol.,* 12: 97–113.

Stein, M. (1998). *Jung's Map of the Soul: An Introduction.* Chicago, IL: Open Court.

Stern, D. (1985). *The Interpersonal World of the Infant: A View from Psychoanalysis and Developmental Psychology.* New York: Basic.

Stern, D.N., Sander, L.W., Nahum, J.P., Harrison, A.M., Lyons-Ruth, K., Morgan, A.C., Bruschweiler-Stern, N., and Tronick, E.Z. (1998). Non-interpretive mechanisms in psychoanalytic therapy: The 'something more' than interpretation. *Int. J. Psycho-Anal.,* 79: 903–921.

Stevens, A. (2015). *Archetype Revisited: An Updated Natural History of the Self*. London: Routledge.

Stone, J. (2016). *The Essential Max Müller: On Language, Mythology, and Religion*. London: Palgrave Macmillan.

Sullivan, B.S. (2010). *Mystery of Analytical Work: Weavings from Jung and Bion*. London: Routledge.

Swan-Foster, N. (2017). *Jungian Art Therapy: Images, Dreams, and Analytical Psychology*. London: Routledge.

Tennes, M. (2007). Beyond intersubjectivity: The transpersonal dimension of the psychoanalytic encounter. *Contemp. Psychoanal.*, 43: 505–525.

Tuch, R.H. (2011). Thinking outside the box: A metacognitive–theory of mind perspective on concrete thinking. *J. Amer. Psychoanalytic Assoc.*, 59: 765–789.

Tuckett, D. (2005). Does anything go? Towards a framework for the more transparent assessment of psychoanalytic competence. *Int. J. Psycho-Anal.*, 86: 31–49.

Tyminski, R. (2022). *The Psychological Effects of Immigrating: A Depth Psychological Perspective on Relocating to a New Place*. London: Routledge.

Urban, E. (1992). The primary self and related concepts in Jung, Klein, and Isaacs. *J. Anal. Psychol.*, 37: 411–432.

Van Eenwyk, J. (1991). The analysis of defences. *J. Anal. Psychol.*, 36: 141–163.

Van Waning, A. (1992). The works of pioneering psychoanalyst Sabina Spielrein – "Destruction as a cause of coming into being". *Int. Rev. of Psychoanalysis*, 19: 399–414.

Vedfelt, O. (2020). Integration versus conflict between schools of dream theory and dreamwork: Integrating the psychological core qualities of dreams with the contemporary knowledge of the dreaming brain. *J. Anal. Psychol.*, 65: 88–115.

von der Tann, M. (1999). The myth of the 'correct' interpretation. *J. Anal. Psychol.*, 44: 57–67.

von Franz, M.L. (1970). *Interpretation of Fairy Tales*. Dallas, TX: Spring Publications.

von Raffay, A. (2000). Why it is difficult to see the anima as a helpful object: Critique and clinical relevance of the theory of archetypes. *J. Anal. Psychol.*, 45: 541–560.

Wallerstein, R. (1988). One psychoanalysis or many? *Int. J. Psycho-Anal.*, 69: 5–21.

Wallerstein, R. (1992). *The Common Ground of Psychoanalysis*. Northvale, NJ: Jason Aronson.

Wehr, D. (1987). *Jung and Feminism*. Boston: Beacon Press.

Weinrib, E. (2004). *Images of the Self: The Sandplay Therapy Process*. Hot Springs, AR: Temenos Press.

West, M. (2011). *Understanding Dreams in Clinical Practice*. London: Karnac.

West, M. (2017). Self-disclosure, trauma and the pressures on the analyst. *J. Anal. Psychol.*, 62: 585–601.

White, J. (2023). *Adaptation and Psychotherapy: Langs and Analytical Psychology*. Lanham, MD: Rowman & Littlefield.

Whitmont, E. (1987). Archetypal and personal interaction in the clinical process. In N. Schwartz-Salant and M. Stein (Eds.), *Archetypal Processes in Psychotherapy*. Wilmette, IL: Chiron.

Whitmont, E. and Perera, S.B. (1989). *Dreams: A Portal to the Source*. London: Routledge.

Wiener, J. (2007). Evaluating progress in training: Character or competence? *J. Anal. Psychol.*, 52: 171–183.

Wiener, J. (2009). *The Therapeutic Relationship: Transference, Countertransference, and the Making of Meaning*. College Station, TX: Texas A&M University Press.

Wilkinson, M. (2006). *Coming into Mind: The Mind–Brain Relationship – A Jungian Clinical Perspective*. London: Routledge.

Wilkinson, M. (2010). *Changing Minds in Therapy: Emotion, Attachment, Trauma, and Neurobiology*. New York: W.W. Norton.

Williams, M. (1963). The indivisibility of the personal and collective unconscious. *J. Anal. Psychol.*, 8: 45–50.

Winborn, M. (Ed.) (2014). *Shared Realities: Participation Mystique and Beyond*. Skiatook, OK: Fisher King Press.

Winborn, M. (2017). The colorless canvas: Non-representational states and implications for analytical psychology. In *Anima Mundi in Transition: Cultural, Clinical and Professional Challenges Proceedings of the 20th IAAP Congress – Kyoto*. Einsiedeln, Switzerland: Daimon.

Winborn, M. (2018). Jung and Bion: Intersecting vertices. In R.S. Brown (Ed.), *Re-encountering Jung: Analytical Psychology and Contemporary Psychoanalysis*. London: Routledge.

Winborn, M. (2019). *Interpretation in Jungian Analysis: Art and Technique*. London: Routledge.

Winborn, M. (2020). Liber Novus and the metaphorical psyche. In M. Stein and T. Arzt (Ed.), *Jung's Red Book for Our Time: Searching for Soul under Postmodern Conditions*. Asheville, NC: Chiron.

Winborn, M. (2022). Whispering at the edges: Engaging ephemeral phenomena. *J. Anal. Psychol.*, 67 (1): 363–374.

Winborn, M. (2023). Working with patients with disruptions in symbolic capacity. *J. Anal. Psychol.*, 68 (1): 87–108.

Winnicott, D. W. (1965). Ego distortion in terms of true and false self. In *The Maturational Processes and the Facilitating Environment: Studies in the Theory of Emotional Development* (pp. 140–152). New York: International Universities Press.

Winnicott, D. W. (1971). *Playing and Reality.* London: Routledge.

Wirtz, U. (2020). *Trauma and Beyond: The Mystery of Transformation.* London: Routledge.

Woodman, M. (1992). *Leaving My Father's House: A Journey to Conscious Femininity.* Boston, MA: Shambhala.

Zinkin, L. (1969). Flexibility in analytic technique. *J. Anal. Psychol.*, 14: 119–132.

Index

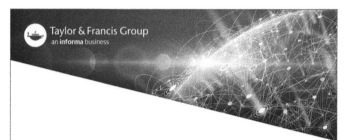